A Woman and the War

Frances Evelyn Maynard Greville
Warwick

BIBLIOLIFE

Photo. Sarony & Co., Ltd.

Frances Evelyn Warwick

A WOMAN
AND THE WAR

BY

THE COUNTESS OF WARWICK

AUTHOR OF

"WARWICK CASTLE AND ITS EARLS," "AUTOBIOGRAPHY OF JOSEPH ARCH,"
"AN OLD ENGLISH GARDEN"

NEW YORK
GEORGE H. DORAN COMPANY

PREFACE

IT is not without serious reflection that I have collected these thoughts in war time to offer in book form to those who may care to read and ponder them. They were written for the most part on the spur of vital moments, when some of the tendencies of the evil times through which we are living seemed to call for immediate protest. I have felt more strongly than ever in the past two years that we are in danger of accepting as something outside the pale of criticism the judgments of those who lead, and sometimes mislead us. The support or hostility of the newspaper press—in some aspects the greatest distorting medium in the world —is still ruled by party considerations. Loyalty or ill-will to the men in office colours all the views of those who praise or blame, and it happens often that a good measure is damned for what is best or lauded for what is worst in it. Again, I have felt that while much of the fighting spirit of the country is subject to army discipline, the tendency of government has been to make helpless puppets of the citizens who remain behind the forces in the field. In the near future, if we would save what is left of our heritage of freedom, and would even extend the comparatively narrow boundaries that existed before the autumn of 1914, we must relieve the press of the self-conferred duty of thinking for us. We must not give our rulers a blank cheque; their best efforts tend more to rouse our suspicions than to compel our confidence.

Judging all the matters dealt with in these pages as fairly and honestly as I can, I have found myself repeatedly in opposition to the authorities. The legislation from which we have suffered since war began, the efforts to relieve difficult situations and prepare for obvious emergencies have savoured largely of panic and can boast no more than a small element of statesmanship. So I have protested and the protests have grown even beyond the limit of these book covers, while an ever-swelling letter-bag has told me that I have interpreted, however feebly, the thoughts, wishes, and aspirations of many thinking men and women. We are on the eve of events that will demand of evolution that it mend its paces or become revolution without more ado. The international crisis and the national makeshifts must have proved to the dullest that the world is out of joint.

I make no claim to traverse the whole ground, modesty forbids, and Mr. Zangwill has accomplished the task in his "War for the World," the most brilliant work that has seen the light since August, 1914. I have sought to point out where and why and how we are moving backwards. I can command no eloquence to gild my words, I cannot pretend to have more to say than will have occurred to every man and woman of advanced views and normal intelligence, but it does not suffice to think; one must make thought the prelude of action. Strong in this belief I have not hesitated to attempt something more than mere criticism. I cannot wave flags, abuse enemies, or extol popular idols; and consequently those who read will please accept these and other limitations.

FRANCES EVELYN WARWICK.

WARWICK CASTLE,
    August, 1916.

CONTENTS

A WOMAN
AND THE WAR

I

KING EDWARD AND THE KAISER

SINCE the war began I have read numerous extracts from the press of Germany and from the contributions of German writers to American papers stating in the most unequivocal terms that the late King Edward devoted his political sagacity to the task of isolating Germany, that he promoted alliances to that end, and that he deliberately sought to compass the destruction of the German Empire.

At first I took these remarks to be no more than the rather unfortunate outpourings of the uninformed, but I have seen of late that they have been repeated with great insistence until there is a danger that they will become an article of faith, not alone in Germany but in other countries where Germans have a sympathetic following. I do not choose as a rule to discuss questions of this kind,

1

I prefer to leave popular error to correct itself, but, having enjoyed the confidence of King Edward before and after he came to the throne, having heard from his own lips scores of times his attitude towards Germany and the Germans, it seems to be a duty to set out the plain truth. I will do so in the endeavour to sweep away one of the most ridiculous and mischievous conceptions engendered by the present evil condition of things.

Had I ever imagined that the present crisis, or, for that matter, any political development of the peaceful kind would have led to the statements I seek to refute, how easy it would have been to jot down the purport of conversations in which high policy was discussed! Fortunately, I have an excellent memory and it is reinforced by letters to which I have access, and I hope to commit the reports that have been spread abroad to the oblivion that is their proper place. I can vouch for the absolute truth of all I have to say, and I am writing with a full sense of responsibility.

In the first place the intimate relations between the English and German courts should be remembered; one of my earliest recollections is of being taken to visit the old Empress Augusta at the German Embassy. This was when I was a child, and I know I went many times, so her visits would probably have been frequent. On my writing-

table is the silver and mother-of-pearl ornament
that was her wedding present to me. Everybody
respected the old Emperor William, and everybody admired the Crown Prince Frederick. When
he married Queen Victoria's eldest daughter, the
Princess Royal, who became, after the death of
Princess Alice, King Edward's favourite sister,
the relations between the two courts could hardly
have been more amicable. Queen Victoria loved
Germany and the Germans, she adored her grandson. In her eyes he could do no wrong, she even
went so far as to hold him up to her eldest son
as a model. On the other hand, the Princess of
Wales, being a Dane, could not forget or forgive
the theft of Schleswig Holstein; her sister the Russian Empress shared her suspicions of German intentions, but I never heard of one or the other originating or encouraging anti-German intrigues.

As the Kaiser grew up towards manhood his
personality was hardly known; his father, the
Crown Prince Frederick, a far more noble figure,
monopolised attention. Beyond the fact that he
was Queen Victoria's favourite grandson nothing
was known about William II. Nobody thought
that he would be called upon to rule before he
was middle aged or elderly; his father's illness
was unsuspected. But if there was no ill feeling
at the English court, it is impossible to say the

same of the court at Berlin. The presence of the Princess Royal was resented; many people believed, or affected to believe, that the marriage had been designed to make Germany politically subservient to Great Britain. As everybody knows, these feelings grew apace as soon as the old Emperor William had breathed his last, and when, a few months later, the Emperor Frederick passed away, the Anglophobia had spread throughout the Court circles and the young Kaiser had been tainted with the Court prejudice against his own mother. He did not treat her well; it is not too much to say that he treated her badly. She, naturally enough, complained to her brother, the Prince of Wales,—I have already said that she was now his best loved sister. He was angry on her account and spoke his mind. Relations between the young Kaiser and his uncle were already strained. I must turn back a little to explain why.

In the early days, when King Edward had arrived at man's estate and married, he sought to take a legitimate interest in state affairs. He was disposed to study and to learn, and sought, not without ample justification, to be admitted to the company of the little group of statesmen who advised the Queen and ruled the Empire. But Queen Victoria would have none of it. She practically refused her son access to the Councils of State, she instructed her Ministers to keep all state papers from him; within the compass of a limited monarchy she was determined to rule alone.

Her eldest son, finding that he was not to be accepted as a worker, decided to amuse himself. If he could not direct public policy he would at least direct fashion, if he could not assist the Foreign Office he could at least enable English Society to take rank among the smartest in Europe. So the Marlborough House set came into existence, and with its rise came the first beginnings of the Kaiser's criticism. There were two grounds for this.

In the first place King Edward's personal popularity was unbounded; wherever he went he charmed women and men, and it was quite clear that he would be a force to be reckoned with in diplomacy, when in the fullness of time he ascended the throne; on the other hand, the Kaiser lacked all the qualities that his uncle possessed in abundance. Hard-working and conscientious, he was petulant, exacting, and uncertain. Naturally, then, he found matter for grievance against the uncle who, seemingly without effort, swayed opinion and enjoyed esteem. Jealousy was the origin of disagreement.

There is another side to the antagonism. The

Kaiser was always a very strict-living, sober-minded man, a model husband and father, honestly representative of the domestic virtues in the highest degree. King Edward, largely by force of circumstances, lived a life of gaiety and pleasure; whatever he did he did thoroughly; as it might not be work, it was play. He raced, yachted, shot, played cards, entertained, visited all his friends, and had a wide field of friendships. Though shrewd, worldly, and quick witted, he made certain mistakes, and these gave his nephew an opportunity that was quickly taken. Perhaps the Kaiser would utter a criticism on the spur of the moment, it would be taken up, magnified, polished, and brought over to King Edward in the finished and augmented state. By the way, I am referring, unless I state the contrary, to the years when King Edward was Prince of Wales. I use his final title to cover all the years with which I am dealing. King Edward had great gifts, and when the time came to turn them to the best account, they were invaluable to his country but, as I have said, he was not infallible. He made mistakes.

Tranby Croft provided one, his friendship for Baron Hirsch provided another; for the Baron, though he may have been a charming man—certainly his wife was a charming woman and a dear friend of mine—was an unscrupulous financier who had accumulated a vast fortune by curious and unclean methods of which the full story cannot be told, and yet for all his faults, he was not an ignoble man, but in some phases of his complex nature an idealist and philanthropist.

Berlin sneered at Baron Hirsch, Vienna was actually shocked, for in the Dual Empire a man is judged by his quarterings, and even if he should have made a huge fortune honestly and lacks quarterings he is less than the penniless, vicious, and brainless person of high descent.

King Edward smiled at the rage and spite of Vienna and Berlin. He remarked to one of his intimates that he could not allow either capital to choose his friends for him, and in order that there might be no mistake about his intentions he accepted an invitation from Baron Hirsch to shoot with him on his great estates at Eichorn. I don't know whether Baron Hirsch asked any Austrians or Germans, certainly none accepted the invitation, and King Edward found, much to his amusement, that all the other guests were Englishmen. He merely laughed, enjoyed his visit, and then, after it was over, visited the Baron in Paris, to the intense annoyance of the Jockey Club there. Perhaps it was not altogether wise to defy the conventions, but of course English Society has never been quite as exclusive as that of Berlin or Vienna.

The Kaiser chafed at his uncle's association with a mushroom financier whose record was only too well known, he chafed too when King Edward spent long hours at Homburg with the Empress Frederick who had a castle there in the days of her widowhood. The love between the brother and sister was very beautiful. She confided all her troubles to him from the early days, for oddly enough when there were family quarrels Queen Victoria sided with her grandson against the Princess Royal, but it is only right and fair to say that the Kaiser reciprocated her affection, and his grief when she passed away was heartfelt. The Homburg meetings were gall and wormwood to the Kaiser and they renewed the old fear of his uncle's popularity. When instead of going to Homburg in Germany, King Edward went to Marienbad in Austria there was still more uneasiness in Berlin's governing circles, for King Edward's extraordinary personal magnetism was known and feared, he was credited with having the power if he chose to exercise it of seriously disturbing the foundations of the Triple Alliance. The Kaiser need not have been uneasy, his uncle did not enter into political conversations.

It will be seen then that the disagreement between uncle and nephew had been little more than a sort of family quarrel intensified by the high standing of both parties. I have heard King Edward speak angrily of his nephew, but only because of the way he treated his mother, the personal gibes and criticisms did not often sting him, he merely said his nephew was suffering from megalomania and had not learned to control a rather unruly tongue. In all the years I have passed mentally in review I do not remember hearing King Edward utter a single sentence of ill-will to Germany.

The Kaiser's visits to England in the earlier days have left no special impression upon my memory. I remember dancing opposite to him in a quadrille at a Court Ball in Buckingham Palace and being present at a dinner-party given for him in a private house. His friends among the ladies of England were the wives of members of the Royal Yacht Squadron; among these was Lady Ormonde. She used to stay at Kiel for the yachting festival, as guest of the Kaiser with her husband who was then Commodore of the R.Y.S.

In all his criticisms King Edward was scrupulously fair. Even in discussing his sister's relations with her son he would add that they were both strong personalities with different sympathies and view-points, and that sustained agreement between them was probably impossible. He admired the Kaiserin frankly, as all must who know the gracious and kindly lady who in her own quiet and unobtrusive fashion has filled her life with good deeds.

Relations between King Edward and his nephew improved immensely when Queen Victoria died. Not only did the Kaiser come over to the funeral, but he seemed on that occasion to have laid aside the brusqueness that had marked earlier visits. All the Court noticed it, and King Edward commented upon it to me with very evident pleasure. The process of improvement in relations started about 1899. Through the Boer War events had been moving towards a reconciliation.

The Kaiser's correct behaviour during the war which his frenzied telegram on the occasion of the Raid had done something to bring about, placated King Edward, and after Queen Victoria's death relations between the two men improved sensibly. The Kaiser either limited his criticisms or saw to it that they were not indiscreetly uttered. The old friendliness was resumed, and things became as they were after the attempt on King Edward's life in Denmark when the Kaiser left Berlin and met the royal train at the frontier station to congratulate his uncle upon his escape and inquire after his health. King Edward wrote to me from Sandringham on his return. After thanking me for a letter and telegram of congratulations, he said that the Kaiser came all the way from Berlin to meet his train at Altona and inquire after his health. He thought that was very kind of the Kaiser.

I remember that the Kaiser's later visits to England were quite a success. King Edward remarked to me, when his nephew was staying at Highcliffe in Hampshire for his health, how greatly he had improved in manner, how courteous and considerate he was, and how much of the old unrest and irritability seemed to have gone. Between King George, Queen Mary, and the Kaiser, relations could not have been more friendly, and when King Edward and Queen Alexandra went to Berlin he thoroughly enjoyed his visit, and told me as much on his return.

How then, it may be asked, shall we account for the Anglo-French convention of 1904, and for the meeting between King Edward and the Tsar at Réval when the foundations of friendship between England and Russia were laid? In Germany it is believed that these arrangements were aggressive in their intention and demonstrated King Edward's hostility. In both cases King Edward, absolutely faithful to the Constitution, followed the advice of his ministers, and did not discuss his personal predilections at all. After the Réval meeting I asked him his view of the political situation, and as far as my memory serves this is what he said: "Germany is our commercial rival, she has a magnificent business aptitude, she might develop with growing riches and a few adventurous statesmen a rivalry of another kind. The Réval meeting, with the French convention, will I hope put an end to the possibility. But nothing has been done that stands in the way of a good understanding between London and Berlin. I believe all sensible men desire peace. We have no quarrel with Germany or any other power."

I may add that King Edward admired Germany almost as much as he loved France. The thoroughness of the German business method, the rejection of everything slovenly in thought and action, impressed him greatly, and he once made a remarkable statement to me. It was in London in the late winter of 1909-10, a few months before he died. He came to tea and talked of German administration. "Do you know," he said, "that if this country could be controlled in the same way, we should be all the better for it? If we could be ruled by Germans just long enough to have our house put in order"—he paused, and added with a laugh—"You know the trouble is that if we once had them we could not get rid of them." This statement was made during our last conversation; I never saw King Edward again, but his

words should be sufficient to show that he was
not animated by an ill-feeling towards the German Empire. They are hardly the words of a man
who plotted against the land ruled over by the
son of the woman who was at once his favourite
sister and most devoted friend.

Age, and an experience of great affairs not to
be excelled by any of his contemporaries, had made
King Edward a sane and philosophic observer.
He possessed very few prejudices, and he never
allowed his feelings as a man to stand between
him and his duties as a king. But if his personal
views had affected political issues it would never
have been to Germany's detriment, for every criticism that I heard him utter over a long period of
years has been set out here. He had a real love
for his French and Austrian friends and a quiet
respect for his German acquaintances. I may add
that King Edward not only hated war and would
have been most reluctant to take any step that
might ensue it, but he regarded people with belli-
cose ideas as fit occupants of asylums. The fine
fabric of civilisation impressed him, and he saw in
war the blind force that would destroy it and leave
the world laboriously and painfully to rebuild.
His real interests lay in the direction of social reform, and he even found the trappings of state,
in which as a rule he took delight, a little heavy

when he realised that they deprived him of the
right of free speech enjoyed by the humblest citizen of the realm. He made it his business to know
what Germany was doing to solve the problems of
unemployment, housing, and factory management,
and in the last years of his life his intercourse with
Liberal statesmen quickened his interest in plans
for the betterment of the class that does the work.
Time out of mind he spoke of what Germany had
achieved in this direction, always with the frank
admiration that only a good sportsman can give
under all circumstances. Far from seeking to bring
war about, it is with me an article of faith that had
he been living in July, 1914, there would have been
no war. The immense personal influence he
wielded would have been thrown into the scales on
the side of peace, he would have reconciled differences at the eleventh hour for he was *persona
gratissima* in every court of Europe, and there is
not among the rulers of Europe one who would
not have listened when he spoke. Those who suggest that he helped to build the pyre upon which
the best and bravest of nearly all the nations of
the world are now being consumed, do but slander
the dead and testify to their own ignorance.

II

THE GREATEST FIGHT OF ALL

In his famous essay on Mr. Montgomery's poems Macaulay speaks of the degradation to which those must submit who are resolved to write when there are scarcely any who read.

It seems a little idle to suggest that two years of war have availed to reduce readers to vanishing point; indeed, editors and publishers of daily and weekly papers testify to an increase of circulation. Paper is harder to obtain than readers; the cause of trouble is that the written word is all of one kind. The love of sensation, strongest amongst those whose mental equipment is of the slightest, is being sedulously catered for, the townsman requires tales of the slaughter of his enemies to give a flavour to his breakfast, his lunch, and his dinner.

Even the countryman, who with no more than one newspaper in twenty-four hours must spread sensation over a day, seems to insist upon flamboyant headlines and cheerful tales of slaughter. Mild-mannered folk, who would turn vegetarians rather than help to kill the meat that is set upon

their tables, may be heard enthusiastically calculating the enemy's losses in terms of six or seven
figures, and discussing the hairbreadth incidents
of flood and field as though they themselves carried a more dangerous weapon than an umbrella
and had faced more serious troubles in the normal
day than an ill-cooked meal, an appointment lost,
or a train missed. In short, people who must stay
at home because they are no longer of fighting
age, strength, or inclination, are being encouraged
to act as the audience. Happily, perhaps, for
them, they cannot see the actual performance, but
they can hear about it, and, as a rule, they are
told what their minds are best prepared to receive.
Truth has received instructions to remain at the
bottom of her well or risk court-martial. Life is
reduced to its primitive elements; war, while it dig-
nifies many of those who take an active part in it,
does little more than degrade the constant reader
of papers of the baser and most popular kind. It
is to be feared that the sane view of life is never
the appealing one, the untrained eye can see trees
but never a wood, and the man in the street is
nearest to the editorial heart because his name
is legion, and the advertiser says to him, as Ruth
said to Naomi, "Whither thou goest, I will go."

In the early nineties there was a literary movement of great promise in London; the Boer War

extinguished it; in the last half-dozen years we have seen a brisk effort towards the development of a national or even international social programme; this war may set it back for a generation; War is ever fatal to ideas. Men whose minds were being turned slowly and reluctantly to questions they had been educated to ignore are now concerned with two problems—winning the war and making good the injuries it has entailed. The increased taxation, the business losses, seemingly irrecoverable, will develop a certain natural hardness of fibre, and there is a danger that the social movements, slow in times of prosperity, will halt in the times to come.

The season of trouble for those "resolved to write" is upon the publicists of the social reform movement. They must be prepared for hard knocks and for all the arts of misrepresentation and vilification. The general reader will first denounce, then ignore and finally listen to the survivors of the common-sense crusade. The people who start to state facts will be the leaders of a forlorn hope, and our brave fellow-countrymen did not face as great an odds in the retreat from Mons. A fight for the universal reduction of armaments and for the remodelling of the existing system of government will be met by indignant cries for conscription and less freedom. The ubiquitous hand

of the German will be traced in every line that
pleads for toleration, good will, and the removal of
all autocracies under whatever name; any suggestion of a return to Christian teaching will be denounced as the highest immorality. There are
many who hold that a conscript Army and a larger
Navy would have saved us from this war; they
cannot see that we should have done no more than
postpone the evil day until it dawned upon Europe in a still greater magnitude of evil, if this be
possible, and that our commercial class, impeded
by forced service, would have been unable to provide the means to pay the bill. The ulcer of European armament has burst at last, and the remedy
proposed for the debilitated body of the Western
World will be a still larger ulcer to take the place
of the one that demanded so much labour to feed
and so much life-blood to cleanse it.

In the same way the effort to make democracy
articulate, to raise the standard of the national
intelligence, will be fiercely resisted by those who
believe that the way of the world in the past must
be the way of the world in the future. The attempt to improve upon the methods of our fathers
is tolerated in the worlds of science, medicine, and
commerce, the innate conservatism of government
is sacrosanct. To educate millions of able-bodied
men, not to the fighting pitch but beyond and

above it, will be denounced as high treason, and
will be opposed by autocracies, bureaucracies,
cannon-makers and publicans alike. A rise to the
heights of sanity is, must be, the death of vested
interests, and every force to the hands of authority will be employed to check the dreaded movement. According to a well-established formula,
the method of attack will be to denounce very bitterly suggestions that have never been put forward
and principles that have no adherents. In this
way issues can be confused and obscured.

To be drunk with victory or dazed by defeat
is to be particularly sensitive to the more brutal
cries of war. The victor desires the full reward
of good fortune, as Germany did in 1871; the van-
quished nurses revenge, as France has done ever
since the end of the struggle that found her so
ill-prepared. Counsels of moderation are declared
to be inadmissible until the *status quo ante* has
been restored, and every force that makes for the
spoliation of the simple by the worldly wise takes
the field against common sense. The appeal of
the dead is forgotten by all living save the woman
whose mission it is to raise another generation for
destruction; the lessons of history cannot be re-
called by those who have never learned them.

Against all the difficulties outlined here, and
many another that need not be set down, a small

body of men and women, inspired by a great ideal, must labour in every country that has seen war or even realised its significance. They must speak and write in the face of fierce opposition and contempt, for war has swept away many of the landmarks they had already set up, together with many of those who had learned to regard them; they must face the truth that many a genuine altruist, shocked unutterably by the revelations of the war, is a little ashamed of his earlier altruism and anxious to forget its existence. They must be prepared for a certain coarsening of the nation's moral fibre, for a long-lived return to the more brutal outlook associated with the Napoleonic era. In some countries revenge will have become an article of faith, in others suspicion will be a no less dominant factor. The whole mental currency will have suffered debasement, and it will be difficult for some vices to be recognised as anything worse than virtues enforced upon a nation by the hazard of war.

If the truth about the whole conflict that has laid waste so great a portion of the civilised world could be ascertained and agreed, the difficulties would tend to disappear, responsibility would be fixed. Unfortunately, agreement is beyond the generation's reach; we may remember that there are many who still regard the seizure of Silesia by

Frederick the Great as a genuine expression of Prussia's mission, and that history is written to suit the country to which it is intended to appeal. Limitations, whether geographical, political, or social, are the sworn foes of truth, and in the effort to remove them an appeal to international common sense affords the best hope of success.

For many of the world's thinkers who stay at home to-day, neither physically fit to fight nor financially able to succour distress, there is this great work waiting to be done. They cannot fight soldiers, but they can fight rancour, malice, and uncharitableness. They cannot fill hungry bodies, but they may help to feed starved minds. They can bring a light to those who walk in darkness and make articulate the thoughts that stir many a heart and brain. They can give courage to those who fear the sound of their own voices and have not the strength of mind to say the words that may not be spoken without offence to the unthinking. When fighting is over—and it will pass, as all tragedies must, though it seems to fill a lifetime while it lasts—the greatest questions of strife will clamour for a wise solution. People write glibly about the war that is to end war, but let us remember that this issue depends not upon statesmen but upon the democracies of all the combatant and neutral countries. What we want is a

modern Peter the Hermit or two in every country of Europe, to preach the crusade of Christi-
anity and to bring home to the world at large the
price of war. There is no material reward for
this service, and even recognition is likely to be
posthumous; the courage required is of the fine
kind that moves alone over uncharted ground. But,
just as a kingdom at war calls for men to man
the trenches and face annihilation with the smiling
cheerfulness that robs death of half its sting and
all its terror, so a return of peace calls for its heroes
of thought to do battle with all the evils that make
it possible for men who have no quarrel to assem-
ble in their millions for mutual destruction.

The whole system of government that makes
these conditions and must be indicted for them is
rotten to the core, but it is enthroned in power,
and will not deal lightly, or even justly, with those
who assail it.

Against this hard truth we have to remember
that every evil that has been subdued since the
dawn of history has been fought in the first instance
by one man or a handful of men. If we have only
a small proportion of thinkers to-day we have more
than there were of old time, when the simplest
education was the advantage of the few. Pagan-
ism was a more terrible force than militarism in the
years of the advent of Christ, and it was over-

thrown by the labours of one man and his tiny following. To-day democracy is all powerful, if and when it can be taught to open eyes and ears. Those who will undertake the perilous task may make this war, whatever and whenever its termination, a fruitful thing for the generations to come, while, on the other hand, if the lessons are not read aright, we may look to pass from tragedy to tragedy, until all civilisation is submerged.

III

It is hard to pierce the thick cloud of cant in which, as a nation, we are all too apt to shroud ourselves. I do not think we are hypocritical, although that charge is laid to our door by all our ill-wishers, but I do believe we are hopelessly conventional, and seldom muster up the courage necessary to call a spade a spade.

I have been re-reading of late, the endless comment upon the drink legislation, some of it frankly inspired by publicans and sinners—I mean distillers—some of it the pure outpouring of cranks, most of it prejudiced, or uninformed, or both. We deplore drunken habits, but when Sir Cuthbert Quilter tried to persuade Parliament to pass a Pure Beer Bill he met with no success. The worst crimes against the person, the common and criminal assaults on women and children, are largely due to drink, and of this drink raw and crude spirits are the worst part; but we do nothing to protect our poorer classes from the poison. To introduce "square face" gin among the black popu-

24

lation of some of our possessions is a deadly offence, the punishment is heavy, swift, and certain, but to poison the workers of our great manufacturing centres is business, and many quite worthy people believe that "when Britain first at Heaven's command arose from out the azure main" it was to do business, and as much of it as possible. Naturally it follows that the fight against cant is all the harder because most of us do not recognise cant when we hear it. I remember how when temperance legislation was first mooted as a war measure many friends who can afford to buy pure French wines and spirits of great age and mellowness solemnly assured me that temperance legislation is mere foolishness, and that they themselves are living proofs that moderation, good health, and a wise activity march hand-in-hand.

But of late years a certain number of women of all classes have been drinking more than is good for them, and since the war broke out the working women's temptations in this direction and the opportunity to indulge them have grown side by side.

The majority of working women are as sober as the majority of every class, but, though there are thousands of temperate women, they are matched by thousands of intemperate ones, the number has grown apace, and I feel they should be saved from themselves. The sober classes cannot resent restriction. It leaves them where they were. The intemperate classes may resent restriction, but it remains necessary in their own interests.

I don't suppose many people read Harrison Ainsworth's novels to-day, but I remember a striking passage in "Jack Sheppard," where Mrs. Sheppard justifies herself to her friend Wood, the carpenter, who has told her that Gin-lane is the nearest road to the churchyard. It is worth quoting—

"It may be; but if it shortens the distance and lightens the journey I care not," retorted the widow. . . . "The spirit I drink may be poison—it may kill me—perhaps it is killing me, but so would hunger, cold, misery—so would my own thoughts. I should have gone mad without it. Gin is the poor man's friend—his sole set-off against the rich man's luxury. . . . When worse than all, frenzied with want, I have yielded to horrible temptation and earned a meal the only way I could earn one . . . I have drunk of this drink and forgotten my cares, my poverty, and my guilt."

The working women whose husbands are at the war have many excuses. They are deprived of their husbands, and—though there is no need to emphasise the point it cannot be overlooked—their lives are a drab monotony of toil, their surroundings are often of the most unfavourable description, the only restraint that can reach them is self-restraint, and their training has done little to provide it. The public-house offers companionship, a brief surcease of anxiety, light and warmth. Many are enervated by much child-bearing, worn out by much house or factory work. They meet temptation and succumb, but let us remember that in classes removed from the same form of temptation there is no lack of intemperance. A very small dose of bad spirits is enough to provide the cheap anodyne some are seeking, and under the influence of drink they are apt to lose their self-respect. The craving for drink grows with what it feeds on, and in all too many cases the hold upon self-respect falters and is lost. We have sent very many men to the war, but enough and more than enough remain behind to take advantage of women who have lost all or even a part of their normal control.

In touch with serious workers in many of the fields of endeavour that make brief oases in the deserts of industrialism, I know that both drink and prostitution have increased since war began, and I know that drink is the great support of prostitution, and that thousands of women of the class we must pity most have a natural sense of shame that drink destroys. If the demons of ruin

—gin and whisky—had not been busy pouring gold into the national treasury, day by day and year by year, they would have been exorcised long since. But business is business, and the gentlemen whose activity corrupts the country can always talk of freedom and liberty, and declare to thunders of applause that Britons never shall be slaves. The possibility of being free to be a slave to drink never occurs to them, or if it does they forget to mention it.

But while I welcome legislation that will tend to keep women sober, and believe that our sex stands in need of more sobriety by reason of its sedentary life, I am far from thinking that the law that is good for women is necessarily good for man. The conditions are altogether different. The self-respecting artisan and skilled worker drink less than ever they did. The men who are doing the country's work to-day in all the armament manufacturing areas need a stimulant, need it far more than the prosperous City man, the real toper of our times. He will drink champagne and whisky with his lunch, and, having had quite enough of both, will damn the working classes for being given to the use of intoxicants. I have been through some of those great works in the north, where labour at and round the furnaces is unremitting, and where to-day the pace has been in-

creased to the extreme limit of physical power.
To preach temperance to the armament worker is
an absurdity; if he is not to be stimulated according to his needs his hours will need to be greatly
diminished; it is impossible for him to give out
unless he takes in.   Why, in the name of all that
is sensible, should he not have that which will help
him?   Why should he have remained so long at
the mercy of cheap, vile spirits that are a more
or less effective poison?   Why should he be at the
mercy of the people who, having little hard work
to do, can thrive comfortably upon lemonade and
barley water?   The manufacturers spare no pains
to obtain the very finest material for their own
work; if it is necessary to spend a few or many
thousands of pounds upon new plant the money is
forthcoming without a murmur.   Does it pass the
wit of these sapient people to give to humanity
a little of the thought they give to raw material?
Can they not see that the best and purest drink
that the new regulations permit is within reach
of the workers, and that the rest is out of reach?

It has long been the custom of the capitalist class
in normal times to give the workman bad drink
with one hand and to raise the other hand with
an expression of holy horror against the sin of
drunkenness, quite ignoring the truth that the
quality, rather than the quantity, that people drink

is often the deciding factor—that every class
drinks, and that if the vice looks worse in one class
than another it is because the poorer the man or
woman, the viler the alcohol supplied to them.
There are so many excellent people who preach
temperance and live on the dividends of drunkenness, there are so many who believe that a reasonable excess in matters of drink is a form of
manly virtue, and there are yet more who believe
honestly in moderation, and do not see that their
good brand of claret, burgundy, or brandy should
be denied to them, seeing they have never abused it.

For myself, I drink a glass of good wine; failing that I am content with pure water. If we
could give our working classes nothing but the
best, and at a price within their means, I should
look askance at legislation, of whatever kind; but
I recognise the old truth that the destruction of
the poor is their poverty, and that the working
man and woman have always been penalised, and
will continue to be, until Government recognises
its responsibilities, and rides its supporters of the
drink trade with a very tight rein.

Above all I feel that the new legislation that
has first restricted and then diluted the working
man's drink must not be regarded as an isolated
instance, but as part of the vast changes that the
war will ensue. The working man will not forego

his legitimate refreshment; it is for the Government to see that it is pure and reasonably harmless. Good beer in moderation will not hurt anybody; bad spirits are the foundation of disease and crime, and, in their silent fashion, are always fighting against the best interests of the State. Sometimes, when I read that the perpetrator of some ghastly crime has been sentenced to death or a long term of imprisonment, with all the pomp and circumstance of our criminal courts, I find myself wondering what poison was administered to him in some squalid public-house, and who among those who rejoice that justice has been done, or vengeance executed, have actually derived financial benefit from the drink that turned a man into a beast. We punish the poor fool with a diseased appetite, we confer some honour or reward upon the prime offender. Then when our enemies say that we are hypocrites we are indignant because of their injustice, or contemptuous of their ignorance, knowing as we do, that God is in Heaven, and that business is business.

Finally, and quite apart from the immediate significance of the drink question, I rejoice in any legislation that will help the working-classes to the full possession of their faculties. If drink helps them to forget intolerable surroundings, insufficient pay, the deprivation of their fair share of the world's beauties, let us be glad that it is taken from them in its worst forms. They will see with clear eyes and with wiser heads, they will no longer be at the mercy of those who pander to their weakness in order to keep them weak. They will enter upon the great struggle that lies before democracy with stronger will and stronger armour. They have surrendered much of their power to the public-house, and the longer its shutters are up the more leisure they will have to see that there are better things in life, the greater will be their determination to share them with the fortunate classes.

There is a time of trouble in store; they cannot be too well equipped to meet it.

IV.

THE problem that faces a State when it sends its best and most virile men to kill and to be killed has certain aspects that few have the courage to handle. For long years, while Europe was an armed camp, the claims of love were admitted amid the demands of war, but now that the dreaded era —which each nation was hurrying through the medium of extravagant armaments and secret diplomacy—has come upon us, we are without a definite plan for securing the continuity of the best elements in the race. If I thought that this appalling war were no more than the prelude to others, I would pray that every woman might be sterile, but hope, our last and eternal refuge against the ills of life, suggests that this most terrible cataclysm will strengthen the hands of democracy and give it the strength to resist further sacrifices in years to come. While the grass grows the horse starves, and while we think of the generation to come, thousands, hundreds of thousands of Europe's best and bravest lie in their hasty graves,

and the cry of Mother Earth is still "they come."
What has been done by our rulers to see that the
fittest shall leave behind them some to take a share
of the white man's burden?

Very little. The men of the middle and upper
classes who happened to be engaged have in very
many cases been wise and patriotic enough to
marry, and their wives have proved themselves as
full of courage as of love. In order to marry, men
have often been obliged to pay the Church an absurd tax, for the Church has shown itself quite
inadequate to the occasion, and trumpery restrictions, meaningless in times of peace and a scandal
in time of war, have not been relaxed. The poor
man cannot afford a special license, and in many
instances has married without the aid or sanction
of the Church. As we know, the State decided
to recognise the unmarried wives of the nation's
brave defenders, a courageous and proper step that
evoked the wildest protests from the narrow-
minded, the "unco guid," and the fanatics who believe that man was made for morality rather than
that morality was made for man. They did not
pause to reflect that our absurd and antiquated
divorce laws are the chief cause of illicit unions,
and that divorce is hardly less hard for the poor to
obtain than are decent housing, warm clothing,
and nourishing food. Happily, in making this con-

cession to the men who are offering their lives to their country, the genius of red tape contrived to assert itself. Hard though it may be to realise, it was for some time a fact that, if a man home on leave married his unmarried wife in order that his children might bear his name, his wife's allowance ceased because he came under the head of those who married after enlisting! The very quintessence of stupidity could have achieved nothing finer.

Unfortunately the majority of those at the front are unmarried. It was considered sufficient to find them physically sound, to vaccinate and inoculate them and then to send them to take their chance. The question of the years to come was never considered. There is no department of War Office or Admiralty that embraces eugenics. I have looked in vain through the speeches of statesmen for a single recommendation to our defenders to marry and leave behind them some pledge of their affection, some asset for the real national treasury that does not consist of gold, as is popularly supposed, but of vigorous men and women as anxious to live for their country as they are willing to die for it. To be sure every wife would have cost the country three pounds a month for the term of the war, and this thought may have given our prudent legislators pause; but I venture to suggest that a wife as a national asset is cheap, even at that price.

The balance has been redressed to some extent, in fashion at once inevitable and unsatisfactory. The billeting of great masses of virile young men in various centres throughout the country, and the opportunities that the new life has afforded resulted in an increase in the number of illegitimate births. I have heard of this from many quarters, and have every reason to believe, in spite of denials, that no district in which large numbers of soldiers have been gathered together will prove an exception to the general rule. Whatever the moral aspect of the question, it cannot be overlooked or ignored. I deplore the promiscuity, though I believe that a wise and daring statesmanship, ready to meet new conditions with new remedies, would have avoided it; but I would like to plead for the foolish mothers, often little more than girls, and for the babes, who in many instances will never see a father's face.

I am not urging humanity in place of morality, for most people lack the moral courage to listen to such a plea; it is rather in the interests of the State that I urge the proper, and even generous, treatment of all those who, before this year is ended, will have entered the world unwanted and unwelcomed. They will be the children of men in the first flush of manhood, of men not lacking in courage and character (or they would not have joined the colours), of men whose fault was that they could not resist temptation in its least resistible form. We must think of the psychology of the soldier who knows that in a few short weeks he may be among the nameless dead, who has embarked upon the greatest of all adventures, and says, "Let me rejoice and be merry, for to-morrow I die." Doubtless in many cases he will return and marry the mother of his child if fate permits, often he will not return, and a soldier's death may well clear a soldier's name.

It should not outrage morality to see that the children, whether they be many or few, born of men gone to the front should be looked after by the State where the mother is unable adequately to provide for them, and it should be possible, too, in cases where the father returns and marries the mother of his child, that such marriage should make the offspring legitimate. It is not a large concession; in many European countries, France included, marriage atones for previous indiscretions, and if this were so in England there would be a much greater tendency to regularise irregular unions for the children's sake. If nothing is done hundreds of young mothers who succumbed to exceptional temptation will be outcasts. Under the

most favourable normal conditions, the lot of the
little one will be hard.   When this hideous war
is over, I would like the regimental officers to put
the facts fairly and squarely to their men, to ask
them to remember the girls they left behind them,
and to be able to assure them, in the name of the
Government, that if they would, on their return,
marry the mother of their child, that child would
become *ipso facto* legitimate.

I am quite sure that many excellent people will
find this plea immoral, that they will say it is con-
doning irregular sex union, that it is removing the
burden from those who have transgressed.   I deny
these suggestions even before they are made.   To
my mind there is more immorality, more glaring
offence to the Creator in one battlefield full of
dead and mangled humanity, than in all the illegitimate children who will have come crying into
our tear-stricken world before the war draws to its
end.   Those who rule over Europe and, being unable to settle their differences, sent millions of men,
who have no quarrel, to deface the earth and
slaughter one another, are morally responsible for
every change in the normal life of mankind.   Those
who replenish the earth are better than those who
destroy it.

War is a monstrous immorality that seeks to destroy the world; the illicit unions, to which I re-

fer in the interest of those who pay the penalty—the mother and the child—are a minor immorality from which, with a little care, a little loving-kindness, and a little fore-knowledge, much good, much deep morality may spring.

There is not much time to lose; there will be much opposition to overcome, and the work of helping the helpless will be widely condemned by those who, having no feelings, are always able to control them. But the effort is worth making, and so I plead here, first, for ample facilities for those who wish to marry before they go abroad; secondly, for the legitimation of the children whose fathers, now at the war, come back and marry the mothers, and, lastly, for some special care of the mother and children themselves.

V

NURSING IN WAR TIME

ABUSES cling to a crisis as barnacles to a ship, and every aspect of war has its own peculiar abuses. While millions do their duty with quiet heroism, there is always a minority that takes advantage, that corrupts others—or itself. Some believe that fraud and foolishness stay at home, that they cannot approach the field of arms, but this is far from being the case.

My thoughts turn back to the South African war, when certain scandals were supposed to have reached their zenith; I look around me to-day, listen to the well-authenticated stories brought to me by relatives and friends, and know that South Africa did not tithe the possibilities of folly and excess. For once I am not pleading for my own sex, I plead for one part of it against the other, for a majority against a minority, for those who are doing what they are paid to do, against those who are voluntary workers. The position comes a little strangely to me when I look at it in this light, but the highly trained, conscientious, painstaking hospital nurse, whose patient heroism proclaims her a true follower of Florence Nightingale, has been exposed to scandalous annoyance for no good purpose and to no useful end, and I feel that I must plead her cause, since she is in the last degree unlikely to plead it for herself.

Society women of a certain class made themselves so notorious in the military hospitals and elsewhere during the South African war that at least one General threatened to send them home and another refused to allow any more to come out. As soon as the greatest struggle of our history started in August, 1914, certain women of means and position proceeded as silently and unostentatiously as was possible under the circumstances to equip hospitals and to set about their self-appointed work. They laboured conscientiously and sought no more publicity than was necessary to enable them to collect money from philanthropists and friends. They did their best, some were already qualified by previous experience, others acquired their knowledge under the most trying conditions possible. They have worked since war began, well content to "scorn delights and live laborious days," some who are near and dear to me have said that they have well-nigh forgotten the old life and the comforts they deemed indispensable only a little while ago. I think it may be claimed for them that they have played a good part, and that in helping others they have not sought to draw attention to themselves or minimise the credit due to the trained sisterhood of love and pity that cheers the wounded and comforts the dying as "The Lady with the Lamp" taught them to do in the far-off days of the great Crimean struggle. They have made many friends and no enemies; the hero of the trenches and the assaulting party has not given more to his country, for both have given their all, the man his strength, the woman her practical sympathy, and both a high degree of physical and moral courage.

Unfortunately there is in London to-day a very large company of young women to whom war was little more than a new sensation. They are not old enough to understand or young enough to be restrained. In normal times they must be "in the movement," however foolish that movement may be, and a war that staggers the old world and the new leaves them very much where they were before. Under the rose they have not diminished their aforetime gaiety, dances and dinner-parties have been the order of the hour. They have not been trumpeted by the section of the Press that delights in recording vain things, but those who view the currents of London's social life know that I am writing the simple truth. There is nothing

to be said; let those laugh who may and can at
such a season, their laughter proclaims them what
they are.

Unfortunately the people I have in mind have
not been content to devote themselves to brainless
frivolity because they must sample every sensation
that the seasons provide, they invaded the sanc-
tuary of the hospital nurse. Scores found their
way to the great London hospitals in town to face
what they were pleased to regard as training; I
have known some who have danced till 3 a.m. and
have presented themselves at the hospital at 8
o'clock! Everybody knows that the training of a
real hospital nurse is a very serious matter, that
it makes full demand upon physical and mental
capacity, and that a long period is required to
bring the seed of efficiency to flower or fruit. The
social butterflies made no such sacrifices; they acquired a trifling and superficial knowledge of a
nurse's work, and then set their social influence to
work in order to reach some one of the base hospitals where they might sample fresh experience.
If they were really useful there it would be un-
kind to offer a protest, but the general opinion is
that they did more harm than good. They sub-
verted discipline, they were a law to themselves,
they were too highly placed or protected to be
called to order promptly, they showed neither the

inclination nor the capacity for sustained usefulness. To sit at the end of a bed and smoke cigarettes with a wounded officer does not develop the efficiency of a hospital.

One heard repeatedly in the early months of the war that this girl or that had gone to the front, and one imagined devotion, self-sacrifice, self-restraint, and a dozen kindred virtues. Unfortunately it is chiefly in the realm of imagination that these virtues existed. For the rest the interlopers wanted limelight, and plenty of it, their pictures flooded the illustrated papers, and to read what was written of them the inexperienced person might imagine that they were bearing the heat and burden of the day, the solitude and anxiety of the night, while in very truth they did no more than search for fresh sensation in an area that should be sacred.

The type of mind that can seek refuge from self and boredom in such surroundings cannot be stricken into seriousness; tragedy cannot reach it. To do a very minimum of work, to attach themselves to the most "attractive" cases, to carry small talk, gabble and gossip into places where so many come to die, these were the main efforts of the young society nurses, and all these outrages were carried on for months on end. The real nurses and sisters were, I am told, bitterly indignant. They asked no more than to be left alone to do their best; but they knew how hard it is to make an effective protest, and they had little or no time to do so. They recognised by reason of their training, the full motive of the excursion into the region of suffering; that craving for excitement, or, in bad cases, erotomania was the motive power. They found their work impeded by the sisterhood of impostors that responds so readily to a fashion of its own making, and their chief hope was that this sensation might pass as so many others have passed, and that the brainless, chattering, thoughtless, empty company, tired of blood and wounds, would find some paramount attraction nearer home.

If there are any who are prepared to think I have overstated the case or have traduced the young women who were lately "somewhere in France," let them find out from their particular heroine how much time she gave to training, how she received her appointment, and how much real hard work she did day by day. That a few have striven hard and nobly I would be the last to deny, but these are not enough either to leaven or purify the mass or to elevate the action of a class that might have been better employed. Let us remember, too, that suffering is always with us, and that even when war is over there will be far too much in all the great centres of our own country. Are these butterfly nurses prepared to remember in the future the profession they invaded? Will they respond to the calls that are made to help, not young, attractive and valiant men, but men, women, and children in every phase of helplessness and hopelessness? I do not think so. There is neither notoriety nor limelight in the sober, serious life of .the hospital nurse and sister. Above all there is a hard and necessary discipline that calls for much moral courage to render it tolerable. Physical courage is seldom lacking either in men or women who are well-bred, and it may be freely granted that a certain measure was demanded even of the butterfly nurses; but there is no redemption in this. To savour the full sense of life without courage is impossible. One might as readily make an omelette without breaking eggs. In this case it is courage misdirected, energy misspent.

I feel very strongly about this scandal—so strongly that I have not hesitated to write what is bound to offend some of my own friends; but there are times when it is impossible to be silent if one would live on tolerable terms with one's self. I feel that in these days woman is called upon to make supreme sacrifices, that what she is giving even now is less than will be required of her later on, that her war record and her record when peace is about to return will be scanned closely and critically by generations of really free women yet un-

born. To know of a blot upon woman's war-time
service record and to make no attempt to erase
it is impossible. The record of the real nursing
sisterhood is brilliant in the extreme. Why should
it be obscured for the sake of a few highly placed
and foolish young women who sought with the minimum of labour to make the maximum of effect?
It is unjust, ungenerous, and altogether unworthy
of the representatives of families that in many
cases have earned their ample honours legitimately
enough.

Great Britain owes more than it can ever re-
pay to the nursing sisterhood; and it is intolerable
that while their silent heroism passes with so little recognition, any girl of good family who as-
sumes a uniform she has not won the right to wear
should pose as the representative of a sisterhood
she is not worthy to associate with, of whose tradition she is ignorant, of whose high discipline and
complete restraint she is intolerant. There are
three classes of women in our midst. The first
earns reward and claims it, the second earns reward and does not claim it, the last claims reward
and does not earn it. Of these classes the real nurse
belongs to the second, and the butterfly sisterhood
to the third. At such a season as this there is
no room in our midst for the last, and it would be
well for us all if authority could spare a moment

from manifold activities firmly and ruthlessly to suppress its future activities. The hardship involved would be of the slightest and the benefit serious and lasting.

VI

TWO YEARS OF WAR—WOMAN'S LOSS AND GAIN

THE long-drawn-out agony of strife is now two years old and, as each day adds its tale of slaughter to the incalculable total, we women may pause in our war work for a moment and endeavour to estimate our own position. We are no longer as we were, "like Niobe, all tears." Niobe, if I remember rightly, taunted the gods, and for this offence all her children were taken from her. We women did nothing to cause our own misfortune; on the contrary, we strove in our little way to promote peace, and to that end, above many others, we sought a hearing in the councils of the nations.

But it was not to be. Our claims were ridiculed or ignored, and now man-made war has swept over Europe like a blight, and we are left to aid our country through the day and to mourn, when the long day's work is done, for our fathers and brothers, our husbands and sons. Yet perhaps the worst is not with those who mourn. The Immortals can sport with them no longer. When the last of Niobe's twelve children had passed, the limits of Latona's vengeance were reached. To have killed the mother too had been a kindness.

The woman whose son or husband has been snatched from her knows the fullness of sorrow, but anxiety for their fate must pass her by, while those of us whose loved ones are on the battlefield would hardly hope for a moment's peace of mind if it were not for the duties that engage our working hours and sometimes earn dreamless sleep. In a wonderful procession that tramped through muddy London under the rain a year ago I saw a great petition by women for the means not only to serve, but to forget.

After all, this claim to national service is no more than was advanced in the old days when access to the heads of the Government was barred and the hooligans of a great city were allowed to give full rein to their impulses. Then our rulers thought they could dispense with women, to-day we are recognised as indispensable. That is all, but it is very much, and it sets me the question that is the title of this brief paper—What has woman lost and what has woman gained?

She has lost much that was dearest to her, much that life is powerless to replace. All the springs of her being have nourished the love that she has given to her dear ones, to the man who was her choice, to the son who fed upon her life. In many cases she has lived almost entirely in her children, for the ties that bind her to the active pleasures of life grow weak in conflict with the powers of maternity. She has forgotten the brief years in which she lived for herself and savoured all the sweets of existence, she has lived in her children, happy chiefly in their happiness, ambitious only for their future and concerned with the struggle for the freedom of her sex less on account of her own generation than on account of that which is to follow. It is woman's *rôle* to give, it is man's *rôle* to take, and custom has staled for him the infinite variety of his taking. And now he has taken so much that made life worth living that she seeks an anodyne for her grief in giving him all that is left to give, the labour of her hands.

This is not only true of the women of England, it applies equally to the women of every belligerent country, friend and foe alike, and it may.be said that between the women of the world there is a common sacrifice and a common sympathy. All have suffered, all must continue to suffer, on a scale that this old world of ours, with all its crimes and tragedies beyond number and beyond belief, cannot parallel. It is this truth that steadies our nerves and strengthens our hearts and sets us looking, past the ultimate sacrifice, to what may lie beyond, not for ourselves but for others.

All that we have has been taken or is being demanded of us. Is there in all the world something to which we may look forward with 'confidence, something that may justify hope? I think there is. Without any sense of pride we may claim that woman has at least vindicated the claims she advanced in those peaceful days that seemingly lie so far behind us. She claimed that she was worthy to play her part in the conduct of national life, that she was in very truth indispensable to it; she was told, by brutal word or brutal deed, that her ambitions outran her capacities. One year of war has given the lie to this assertion. Woman, even before the coming of compulsion, encouraged her dearest to go, if needs be, to their death, in a war for which she has no shadow of responsibility before God or man. Conventions, agreements, treaties, alliances, in all these things she has no share, but as soon as they materialise in war she must pay the heaviest price.

The excitement and glory of a struggle in which the fighter feels that he has surrendered his life to high causes is not for her, she must be content with the pale reflex or with the tragedy. In her heart she may know that man incurs the penalties of his ambitions or bad diplomacy or unpreparedness for upheaval; but those penalties press heavier on women than on men, for, even granting that the love of husband for wife and wife for husband be equal, yet the passion of a mother for her child and her grief when he is snatched from life in the hours when life is unfolding all its possibilities, is something beyond the strength of man to grasp.

But woman has not failed on account of her griefs, she has strangled them—or she has tried to with all the strength that has been given to her—and she has gone out into the market-place and said, "What more do you require of me? Ask and I will give, direct and I will obey." Hers has been the supreme sacrifice, and now at the moment when all that seemed worth striving for had passed, she sees suddenly a fresh horizon, the Pisgah view of the Promised Land.

She realises that man is at last beginning to understand and even to acknowledge her place in the world, that the future cannot repeat the errors of the past, that the day-dawn of her emancipation is visible. This war, reconciling so many differences, rebuking so much pride and bringing so many men and women face to face for the first time in their life with life's actualities, has united all workers, irrespective of class or sex. It is seen now that woman has a part to play in the conduct of the State, and that there are spheres of activity in which women might and must work for the common good. She and man together must build up a new civilisation out of the wrecks of the old one, not only here but throughout the strife-stricken world. Old barriers, time-worn preju-dices, a blind conservatism—what part have these in the mental attitude of nations freed from over-whelming peril?

The soul of my sex would be as desolate to-day as the ruined cities of Belgium, Poland, and Servia, were it not for the certain knowledge that our sacrifice has not been made in vain. We have the right to hope that our share in the work of the world is to be acknowledged at last, and that the spheres of our activity are to be widened. In this way, and only thus, we shall be able, in years that have yet to be, to influence thought and to influence action, to bring a humanizing note into the great chord of life. We shall strive through the sisterhood of women towards the brotherhood of man, and we shall be working among those who will be able to see for themselves what one-sided rule and one-sided domination have done for progress and civili-sation after their slow ascent to a position that at best left so much to be desired.

The women of my generation will sow where they may not hope to reap, but there is nothing new for woman in this experience. It is her mis-sion in this world to sacrifice herself, from the hour when she accepts motherhood until the end. Her happiness is derived from the contemplation of the happiness of others, she lives in the new lives with which she renews the world. She will leave contentedly to others the prizes for which she laboured in years of peace and suffered through the season of war. It will be sufficient for her dimly to foresee the time when those who have replaced her will give birth to sons with no more pangs than Nature demands, and give birth to daughters in the belief that they will not be widowed or fatherless or childless through catastrophes of man's own making.

So it seems to me, looking back at the cruel record of two years, that woman, for all her losses, has gained, that what she has lost is matter for her private sorrow, and what she has gained is matter for universal joy. She has found the uses of adversity, she has accepted self-sacrifice for the sake of those who will be the better able to enjoy the rich fruits of life. In this knowledge she will labour, for the sake of this truth she will persevere with a confidence in the future that no shifting tides of chance can shake. And her watchword in the coming year is, Hope.

VII

CHILD LABOUR ON THE LAND

IT is a commonplace that war brings in its train evils without number, but there are certain ills that are added to the inevitable ones either by greed of gain, indifference to progress or a determination to make profit at the expense of the State. We have in our midst at all times certain people who are concerned only with their own ends, and who regard all the means to those ends as legitimate. War time reduces the measure of restraint that the common sense of the community imposes upon its greedier members. They find and seize their hour when normal conditions are upset. It would be easy to multiply instances, but in writing this paper I am concerned with one only—the employment of children on farms.

To the average man who does not know a swede from a turnip or the difference between sainfoin and clover this is a small matter; to those of us who know the land and its problems, who administer estates large or small, who are morally if not legally responsible for the happiness and well-being of village communities, it is a tragedy.

I can remember hearing my elders talk of the
bad old days when the gang system prevailed all
over England.   The ganger was a contractor of
irregular labour.   He would enter a district in
charge of his wretched company of men, women,
and children, and would supply their labour at fixed
rates to the farmer who needed it.   He charged so
much a day for each hand; he saw to it that one
and all did their full day's work.   They were fed
abominably, housed in barns and out-houses, and
lived in a promiscuity that would revolt a gipsy.
At last even the thick-skinned countryside could
endure the abomination no longer, and the "ganger" disappeared.   It took years for the Legisla-
ture to discover that, apart from the cruelty involved in the custom, it was creating fresh material
for gaols and asylums, that children needed education rather than field labour, that the mothers
could not combine maternity with hard work in the
fields, that if you deprive people of the means of
living decently they will revert to the state of savagery.

The agricultural labourer's struggle has not been
limited to the land.   He has been fighting for
years to raise his miserable wage.   When I was a
girl it was about a shilling a day with "small beer"
of the farmer's brewing thrown in.   It is about 8s.
6d. a day now; but against this the price of necessi-

ties has gone up between 50 and 100 per cent. Saving is impossible, and even the old age pension that lightens the evening of his long day hardly avails to keep him from the workhouse—unless he has a wife of equal age or children who, out of their tiny means, will render a little assistance. He lives in a cottage that, if often picturesque, is nearly always overcrowded; his food and clothing are of the roughest, and for holidays he has Christmas Day and the wet weather, when he may sit at home —at his own expense—for when there is no work there is no pay. But he lives in hope; and sometimes he goes on strike, to the disgust and indignation of his employer, and his children have been getting a better chance in life than he had. They are supposed to be kept at school until they are fourteen. He was rook scaring at the ripe age of ten for a penny a day.

Rural education is a poor thing enough. Children may have to walk two miles or more, in all weathers, to the village school. Their father cannot afford to buy them good boots or a water-proof coat; it is beyond his means to give them nourishing food, and so help them to fight the diseases of childhood; but he feels that something is being done for them, and, as a rule, he does nothing to make them wage-earners before their time. Now they are taken from school two years before an age that the trade unions hold to be insufficient; they are sent on the land to work for a wage of eighteen pence a day, in any weather, on any soil, without the proper clothing and with insufficient food. There they will undersell the rural labour market, they will be robbed of their childhood, they will go without supervision at a time when they need it most. And the Bumbles of our Education Councils have nodded thick, approving heads.

It is hard to write patiently of such retrograde devices, put forward, as all such proposals are, in the name of the country's needs. If these needs be genuine, which I doubt, if there be no adequate supply of female labour to be obtained for a fair price, why should the children of our poorest, the little ones whose physique has never been strengthened by sufficient nourishing food and by the hygiene of the home, be called upon to bear the burden single-handed? Why should not Eton and Harrow, Rugby, Marlborough, Winchester, and other schools without number, serve the national need? The lads at these expensive establishments can at least complete their education after the war, they can carry health and strength to the fields, they can acquaint themselves at first hand with the realities of labour, a knowledge that, with the changing times ahead, will be valuable to many of them who will inherit land in days to come. Will the farmers who are sending to the fields the half-grown children of their ill-paid labourers contribute their own to work by their side? I am sure that the mere suggestion will rouse the wildest indignation; but all the children, whatever their advantage or disadvantage, are British citizens, and it is not too much to suggest that those who have a stake in the country should at least do as much as those for whom fortune provided no birthright. Let us be democratic in deeds as well as words. I am quite sure that, if the doubtful privilege extended to the rural labourer's children were conferred at the same time upon the children of all patriots, the councils would expunge their fatuous resolutions from their minute books; they would make all possible haste to forget them.

But it may be urged that, in pleading for the children, I have overlooked the crying needs of the countryside, that I am ignorant of the real need for labour to deal with the increased area of the corn and for the late-sown spring crops, for it is clear that, as soon as the proposal for universal child labour is made, the scheme falls to the ground.

I am well aware of the existing conditions—what landlord is not?—and I have a remedy for them. It is not a popular one, but I am not searching for popularity. In spite of the genuine sacrifices that have been made by many classes of the community, much more remains to be done. We have all over the country racing stables full of lads who cannot go to the war and of men who have passed serviceable age. Hard work in the fields from April to the time the last corn is under the stack thatch would do them all the good in the world, and, with some knowledge of all classes of horses, I believe that horses would survive and the superiority of the British sires would not be lost.

Having depleted the racing stables, even at the cost of reducing the number of race meetings, I would turn my attention to the golf clubs: their name is legion. What an army of "ineligible" caddies might be recruited for the fields and given the chance of earning a living intelligently! I go so far as to hint that thousands of the elderly gentlemen who still pursue the golf ball might find more useful occupation in ministering to the country's genuine needs.

Let me pass from one monstrous suggestion to another. I would enroll the gamekeepers and the gillies; for once I would leave the wild pheasants to breed as they will and the grouse to work out their own salvation. A desperate remedy, but then our disease is dangerous. We need corn even more than pheasants, and other game birds can look after themselves. There might be an epidemic of poaching, in which case I would sentence every poacher

to three months' hard labour—on the land. We
have in this country to-day hundreds, I might say
thousands, of sturdy middle-aged men who are now
following occupations that, while they are perfectly
reasonable in times of peace, are superfluous, even
derogatory, to-day.

There is yet another class that can be mobilised
to serve the country's need. I would like to see
the last remaining footmen and the valets of middle age allowed to enjoy a summer of useful activity. They, too, may be in their right place at
normal times; now their country needs them more
than their masters do. A little hardship would be
involved, but I do not believe there are many employers of superfluous or ornamental labour who
would, if the matter were put before them fairly
and temperately, place their own petty comforts
before the country's need for food. We hope and
believe that we may rely upon our Fleet to feed
us, but why should we run risks? No war is won
until it is lost, and if by ill-fortune we experienced
a shortage, I do not think that the owners of racing
stables, the renters of shooting and fishing, the
members of golf clubs and the employers of men
servants could acquit themselves of a serious responsibility. If all these sources of supply are
tapped, and it is still found that the supply of labour in the fields is inadequate to the nation's needs,

let us proclaim a national holiday in all the schools of the country, and let the high and the low born, the rich and the poor, seek the fields together. But until all sources of adult labour have been exhausted let us spare the little ones, and in any case let us see that those whose share of the good things of life is smallest are not called upon to endure trials and make sacrifices that we would shrink from demanding of our own children.

VIII

COMRADES

In times when national emotion is deeply stirred it is possible for the close observer to get a glimpse of the main trend of thought. Just as a feather will show the direction of the wind, a word may show the direction of a man's mind. It is on this account that I was deeply moved and greatly stimulated of late by hearing that as the gallant Frenchmen attack the enemy their rallying cry is "Camarades, Camarades!" This is one of the most beautiful words in any language, it is the one by which a nation may rise to the height of its greatest achievement, whether in clearing its beloved land of a hated enemy or clearing its administration of the abuses from which no administration is free. One hardly dares to think of what the world might be like to-day if war had not been needed to establish the wonderful unity the word bespeaks.

There is not on all the earth a more democratic army than that of France, and to-day it is a perfect union, a veritable brotherhood. From the highest General to the humblest "piou-piou" there is but one aim, one ideal, prince and peasant pursue it to the end. One and all know that if success is to be achieved against heavy odds, it is by the help of the real brotherhood, the feeling that the accidents of birth and fortune do not count any longer, that "a man's a man for a' that." Other countries have caught a glimpse of the truth, our own among the number, but it needed French clarity of vision to recognise the truth and crystallise it in a word—a simple word with the mystic number of letters and so powerful that, when it becomes the rallying cry in times of peace for all civilised nations, the evils under which men and women labour will be swept away like chaff before wind.

For many years past I have been convinced that the enemies of mankind are not men. Ignorance, poverty, greed, vice, disease, these are the foes that prey upon all communities, and while those who foster them are of no brotherhood, those who would combat them need no more than brotherhood in order to overcome. War, in which a man makes the supreme surrender, in which he discounts the terror of death and makes purposes splendid by his devotion, reveals the truth even to those who have never thought before. Will brotherhood survive war, or does it need the exaltation born of the greatest of world tragedies to open a nation's eyes—and keep them open?

The history of our civilisation depends upon the answer to this question. Nothing less than brotherhood will enable the nation to face the widespread poverty that already exists, but will not be recognised until peace is restored. There will be very little money left in the countries of combatant nations, and there will be very many needs. The care of the wounded, the maimed and the helpless, provision for the widows and the children of war will come first. Then there are the schools; nothing is more vital to the future generation than education, and few great claims are more in danger of a grudging treatment.

There are two ways of handling a nation's affairs, one is to make the rich richer at the expense of the poor, the other is to make the poor less poor at the expense of the rich. The peaceful solution of the whole problem is found in the battle call of our gallant Allies. If we are "camarades, bons camarades!" we can endure our national privations and scarcely feel them, for we shall all be in the same boat, and it is not poverty that galls but the contrast between poverty and wealth. Down to the time when war began this contrast was ever present, it was becoming one of the great dangers of our time; it has not disappeared to-day, but it is far less noticeable, and as we continue to spend between thirty and forty million pounds a week on

· war, the cases of contrast will tend to grow less and less. I look for the time when men and women will find it as distressing to flaunt riches as the poor find it to display the outward and indisputable signs of poverty. One does not envy even now the state of mind that enables a man to say that he is "doing very well out of this war."

Among "comrades" such a thing would be impossible, the only excuse for making money out of national misfortune is to be found in its wise distribution to alleviate the suffering that war renders inevitable. To amass wealth from the country's needs, to spend it on purely personal ends, to allow an orgie more terrible than the Black Death to fill private coffers, this surely is the negation of brotherhood, and those who do it are the outcasts of civilisation, even though they purchase palaces and peerages and every honour that unscrupulous Governments vend in semi-privacy. How will the men who have thrown their lives into the scale tolerate the men who trafficked in the necessities of life, or the implements of death, and demand the high places as a reward for successful huckstering? They will not lightly reckon them in the ranks of the "comrades"; in a world founded on brotherhood there will be no place for them. If there be a place in the near future perhaps it will be the nearest lamp-post. Stranger things have happened.

Sometimes I think we could afford to lose this war, or, at least, not to win it, if the Frenchman's battle call could become the rallying cry of all parties and all grades in this country.   Much as I loathe war and all it stands for, I feel that an instant victory would have been very bad for us, while a success won by waiting must at least purge our national life of the grosser elements.   The mingling of high and low, of rich and poor, the price of strife demanded of each and all, the community wrought by suffering and by heavy loss, all these things are salutary for a nation grown plethoric by prosperity. It will not greatly matter if we lose half the world and gain our own souls, for the simple reason that an England wide-eyed, clean-limbed, and efficient could yet achieve and retrieve, while an England besotted by sloth and bemused by riches can only endure until the advent of a stronger and more determined race.

Whatever our destiny, whatever the future holds in store, we shall be happy indeed if we can face difficulties, dangers, privation, or supreme victory with the cry of "Comrades!"   When war came, this country was fast sinking towards civil strife, drifting for lack of the spirit of good fellowship.   A few masters, innumerable men, industry organised into limited liability companies that the human touch, the community between employer and employed,

might cease, the wealth of the country divided on
lines that gave 90 per cent. to a tenth of the population and divided the remaining one-tenth of the
wealth between 90 per cent. of the people who create it,—these conditions were making for a social
upheaval of bloodiest kind. Education starved, an
infant mortality greater than the present waste of
war, discontent, ill-feeling, class hatred, all these
things were, all these things may be again, but not
if the cry of "Comrades!" is taken up.

Whether we win or lose, I see civil unrest inevitable, for this war has sounded the death-knell
of the old industrial, social, and political conditions.
Nothing within the range of possibility can leave
us just where we are, and worse than the struggle
with an enemy is the struggle with a friend.
Though I hold all war to be fratricidal, yet civil
war must ever remain the worst form of it. As
soon as the old problems force their way again to
the fore the danger of civil strife becomes imminent, and let us remember that the working classes
that come back from war will have forgotten what
fear means. It seems to me that salvation lies in
the Frenchman's fighting cry, that in giving his
brothers a lead he has offered a lead to civilisation. He has shown us how to make the inevitable
changes peacefully.

Idealism is out of fashion to-day because—let us

not burke the truth—our idealists were deceived about Germany's intentions, and those in high places unconsciously misled the people. Yet let us cling to our ideals, for they may prove our best possession, and let us realise that the cry of "Comrades!" may, as years pass and the old bitterness dies away, extend across frontiers and bind in a common brotherhood the sons of the men who sought to destroy one another. Such is the potency of a word that revivifies life, laughs at wounds and disarms death. It sums up the aspirations of the greatest reformers and social workers of old time, of the men, from John Ball to William Morris, who strove for England. Only the French people, with their innate sense of selection, could have picked upon a word that can sum up the best of the ideals of the human race. We are their debtors for it, and there is no nobler way of paying the debt than by developing the cry until it resounds from one end to the other of our Empire. It will renew our youth, it will destroy many of the old evils that were even worse than war, it will realise the ambitions of men who lived and died for England in times of peace, when there is no reward for social heroism other than the consciousness of a supreme effort made on behalf of people one may never see, people who will never understand.

If the future of the world is with sane, wide-eyed democracies; if man is to be free to do the world's work and develop human destiny without turning aside at the bidding of kings and rulers; if humanity, with its common lot and destiny, is to develop the spirit of brotherhood that makes life beautiful,—we could have no finer rallying cry than France has offered. I do not believe that the country capable of originating and responding to it can be beaten by sheer weight of numbers; I feel that it is one of the world's assets, and that somewhere in the background the Great Force we strive to comprehend, and, comprehending, to worship, will guard it against ultimate defeat. To doubt this were to believe that the race is to the swift and the battle to the strong, and that the man who can invent the most efficient machinery can dominate God's world. Such a belief is to me the most unpardonable form of atheism. This world was not made, was not populated, was not instructed, that soulless machinery might hold it in thrall at last. The French know this, hence the battle cry that thrills me as I write.

IX

IN the great gale that sweeps over Europe the few rags that hide the nakedness of monarchy flutter like scarecrows; I find myself watching for the gust that will reveal to the gaze of the least discerning what a dangerous and ridiculous thing the bare bones of kingship have become.

England has filed the teeth of the serpent, it can bite no more—the phrase is Swinburne's not mine. We keep our kings as we keep the Regalia in the Tower, well housed and well looked after, and between the ruler and the ruled there is a pleasant, but indefinite relationship. Kingship for us is the focus of patriotism and loyalty, but we should not go to war because the house of Guelph were jealous of the house of Hapsburg, or on bad terms with the house of Hohenzollern.

Those German pundits who believe that King Edward made the Anglo-German war have never grasped our national attitude toward monarchy, or King Edward's ungrudging recognition of the merits of the German people.

72

With us monarchy is an abstraction, very little more.

There was a time when it was supposed to be the fountain of honour, but politicians have fouled the waters so much and have bought and sold honours so unblushingly that modern royalty would be a little ashamed to father so large an illegitimate progeny. A business nation, we have a fixed price for everything. We pay our kings so much a year, and if they exceeded their allowance the State would hesitate to make up the deficit. Baronies, baronetcies, knighthoods and the rest have their fixed price, generally, though not invariably, payable to the party whips who consider themselves morally bound to deliver the goods.

When we were on the brink of war in 1914, M. Poincaré wrote a touching letter to King George, such as an old-time king might have sent to a brother sovereign. King George signed a reply that has been published—one would wager that nothing save the signature involved his heart or his pen. It was no more than the letter of a greatly harassed minister who was trying to think while he balanced himself on a high and unstable fence. Here was ample evidence that all who run might read of the final surrender of the monarchy, and incidentally, of the desire of England to maintain peace.

Nobody wants more than the shadow of kingship in this country. Everybody with more than
the most perfunctory knowledge of history has realised that half the wars of the world have been
fought for the gratification of kings, and most of
the others have been waged in the name of religion,
i.e. to demonstrate the superiority of one orthodoxy
over another. Slowly, and at such a sacrifice as
the world may well shudder to contemplate, we have
come within sight of the end of religious strife.
There remain wars of kingship, the present one
is little more than that.

Down to a few years ago the old gates were still
standing at Temple Bar to divide the City from
Westminster. At Warwick Castle the drawbridge
is still raised every night. In some of the cities
of Southern Spain watchmen, armed with spears
and oil lamps, still proclaim the time of night and
the state of the weather. The "Miracle" of the
Sacred Fire remains an annual spectacle at Easter-
tide in the Church of the Holy Sepulchre that is
in Jerusalem.

The world, as though conscious of the ugliness
of so much that is modern, still clings to old cus-
toms and institutions even when they are absurd.
That is why autocratic kingship survives.

The house of Hapsburg has been ruling in Europe since the thirteenth century; in Germany as

well as Austria for part of the time; the rule of the Hohenzollerns dates from 1871. A German, Count Berthold, is said to have originated in the eleventh century the house of Savoy that governs Italy. In Spain we find the ubiquitous Hapsburgs and the Bourbons sharing rule. A Hohenzollern is in Rumania, and on the distaff side in Greece. A Princess of the Hohenzollern house was the mother of King Albert of Belgium; Ferdinand of Bulgaria has Coburg and Bourbon blood.

A system of inter-marriage has retained power in the hands of a few houses, but nature is ill-disposed toward inbreeding and has scourged the cunning of kings with insanity and disease. While democracy has grown in stature and in vision, while it has been claiming its own place in the sun, the small privileged class has diminished physically, mentally, morally, but still clings desperately to place. There are a few brilliant exceptions, Albert of Belgium for example, but Hapsburgs, Hohenzollerns, Coburgs, and Bourbons are, generally speaking, no longer qualified from any standpoint to rule the destinies of free peoples. They are a little better than well-connected anachronisms, avid of the power that is passing from them and ready to offer any sacrifice that their subjects are capable of making in order that their time-tarnished prestige may shine again.

The wishes of their people are the last thing to be considered by autocratic monarchs. They will not stand in the scale against the interests of their relatives, and in the courts of Europe it is hard to find a ruler who is not a cousin of some sort to all his fellow-sovereigns. Jealousy, ambition, ill report, dyspepsia, disease, dementia, any one of these evils if it be backed by greed, may avail to plunge innocent nations into the hell of war. Forces that sway a republic are powerless in an absolute monarchy or in one where servility and orthodoxy strive hand in hand. There are few European rulers who have half the sagacity of the chief advisers whom they may override at will. They are not as a rule men and women of great culture, few if any have ideas that belong of right to the twentieth century, their function has outgrown them, and the reverence they demand and receive is founded very largely upon ignorance and superstition.

To plunge Europe into war for purely personal ends has always seemed in the eyes of kings a reasonable action. Frederick the Great admitted that he started the Seven Years' War by stealing Silesia from Austria for "glory," and the records of Spain and Austria are full of similar crimes.

Now that Europe has been shaken from base to

summit, will the sober manhood of the twentieth century allow the present system to endure?

On the other hand, I see a great movement toward giving kingship a fresh lease of life, toward perpetuating secret diplomacy and developing clericalism. But men who have stood face to face with the living God should decide to worship henceforth after the inclination of their own hearts. Elderly gentlemen of conservative tendencies are already writing to warn the public that, however awful the chaos now prevailing, democratic rule would have made it worse. I welcome such warnings, for they are a proof that the upholders of tradition are at last aware of the slippery places over which they must so shortly tread.

If the democracy can see the truth, if its eyes refuse to be dazzled by flags, medals, and uniforms and its ears will convey each plausible speech to the brain for sober analysis, this war will not have been waged in vain.

I hold in all seriousness that it is a strife of kings. Gladstone once asked anybody to tell him how the Austrian Empire had been of any service to humanity. The aggregation of uncongenial nationalities has been kept together for the greater glory of the effete house of Hapsburg, a house whose true history, even since Kaiser Franz Josef came to the throne, could not be printed. The genius of the

German people, their magnificent education, stern discipline, tireless industry and full nurseries were conquering both hemispheres, but that was not sufficient. Unless the German could pay tribute to the house of Hohenzollern and increase the Imperial prestige, progress was an egg without salt to the palate of the Potsdam hierarchy.

The fruits of forty years of labour and a generation of child-bearing were flung into the scale that the Hohenzollerns might stand more directly in the limelight.

The people whose blood was to be spilt, whose wives were to be widowed, whose wealth was to be squandered, were wilfully deceived and were driven to war as the Pharaohs drove their warrior-slaves.

Their awakening must come, and with it let us hope a further accession of strength to the Social Democracy that is the best hope of Germany.

We know that neither England nor France desired war, that Russia, whatever her interest in the great Slav-Teuton controversy, was not ready for it, and the worst to be said of the Allied Powers is that, conscious of an enormous menace, they united to destroy it. But every thinking man knows that without the ambitions of a few soldiers, statesmen (so-called), and officials this war had never come about.

I have often compared the position of republics

with that of monarchies and have cited the American Republics. The United States live in peace, even the South American States, with their mixed population, their Spanish, Portuguese, German and Italian blood, are seldom found long at strife.

Royalists have spoken to me glibly about the corruption that is said to be inherent in republics. It is about the only charge they can formulate, and the reply is obvious. In republics corruption is hard to hide, it comes to the surface and is visible to all. In monarchies corruption, no less rife, is hard to expose; all the avenues to light and free speech are closed.

Your republic brings character and brains to the top; your monarchy makes statesmen of courtiers and sycophants, men who will bow the knee to the Baal of the hour.

A republic is open to the air of heaven. A monarchy is a garden enclosed, richer in rank weeds than flowers. If Germany had been a republic, the Social Democrats could have learned the truth and acted upon it; had Austria been a republic, giving equal voice to all the interests it affects to represent, sympathy with the Slavs would have kept the rulers from their disastrous attempt to reduce Serbia to the status of a vassal kingdom.

Kings have served their time. The ruler who rode to war at the head of his troops, who could handle the heaviest sword or battle-axe, who was both the ruler and judge of his people, belongs to a bygone era. His last *raison d'être* passed with the era of industry and rapid transit. He became an anachronism when people began to realise that life is a gift to be wisely used, and that racial antagonisms may be cured or dispersed by close relationship. It is for kings and for kings alone that millions of men who have no real quarrel have slaughtered one another under conditions of horror that make description inadequate. Until we understand that simple truth that the natural inclination of civilised man is to live on friendly terms with his neighbour in spite of all divisions of boundaries, whether of place, blood, or religion, civilisation will be rendered null. Kings have ceased to represent their people; the time has come when the people can represent themselves.

Unhappily they do not yet recognise their own power, and nothing is farther from the wishes of Europe's tottering dynasties than that they should do so. Education, their first aid to emancipation, has been grudgingly conceded. Representation is in its infancy and is hedged round with so many safeguards to royalty that in many countries it is still struggling for effective existence. For all our brave talk Europe is still in its first youth, but the tragedy through which we are passing may yet serve to stimulate its growth as surely as the blood shed on its fields will yield return in the fruits of the earth.

Will democracy rise from the conflict not only strong but determined? Will it carry destruction to the source of destruction? Will it assert its inalienable right to the fruits of peace, progress, and utility? I pray that it may, but I do not disguise from myself the enormous difficulty of the task. Demos is yet so unskilled, so easily flattered, so readily deceived, he will be met by men who have all the traditions of humbug at their finger tips; indeed, these traditions are almost their sole inheritance and equipment.

Yet, "all that a man hath will he give for his life," and the democrat will not only be fighting for his own but for his children's lives and for the well being of the human race. He will have faced death, and will have realised that though man may die but once, the condition of rule that makes war possible makes the doom recurrent with every generation. He should know that the old traditions of rule are in the melting pot, and though all the forces of reaction will labour to shape them again as of old, it is in his power, if it is in his will, to frustrate their action.

The United States looks to have a voice in the making of peace. Doubtless it will do useful work, but I cannot conceive of any better task for the great republicans of to-day than to give the western world the lead that may help it most of all. Most of them have seen monarchies at their best and worst; all of them are patriots; they know what republicanism has done for their own fair land. Will they stand silent now while the western world is faced by the danger of the perpetuation of a *régime* that has little or nothing to justify it? If they do, they have missed the finest possible chance of spreading the light that shone upon them when the Declaration of Independence was signed one hundred and forty years ago.

With the end of the war, if it does not result in the hegemony of Germany, in which case liberty will be no more than a name, all manner of schemes for the regeneration of Europe will be afoot. Few, if any, will go to the root of the evils that have devastated Belgium, Poland, and a part of France. It is safe to say that the disposition to bring about sweeping reforms will not find ready expression. We are all too close to events over here, the blessing of a clear, serene outlook is denied us. The United States has stood far above the turmoil, it has seen more of the truth than has been visible to any combatant nation, it can survey the whole situation sanely.

It seems to me in these circumstances that the

greatest republic of the world has a serious duty, a grave responsibility. It has thriven on a gigantic scale without patronage or privileged classes, without titles, without such honours as are merely honours in name. Freed by the Atlantic from the domination of Europe, it has grown in power and given its citizens a life removed from the worst anxieties that beset the Continent. It knows what kingship in its absolute aspect has cost Europe, and it embraces within its wide domain the children of every European nation; they dwell side by side in peace and amity. The freedom enjoyed by the republic would not be bartered for the wealth of the world, for that freedom is the secret of its eternal youth, its boundless energy, its untrammelled progress.

There are men in the States to-day, men I am proud to number among my friends, who might speak in due season the words that would encourage Europe in the only fight that can rightly engage all nations, the fight against the curse of kingship. We who know how much this fight is needed, who have seen in the great republic how it welds together the most diverse faiths and nationalities, believe that nothing but kingship divides man from man in Europe and fills every frontier line with the instruments of death.

All the sympathy of the best elements in the

United States is with suffering Europe to-day, but it cannot be expressed without the use of words that will sound harsh to some, impertinent to others, startling to all.   Yet these words will not fall upon deaf ears.   They will bring hope to many for whom the future is utterly dark, who believe that the forces of reaction will strive desperately to overcome democracy and that democracy needs prompt help if it is to survive.

Granting that America has the right to be heard when the time comes for the re-establishment of peace, she has the right to deliver the message of her own hundred years of freedom.   Is it too much to hope that she will rise to the height of this supreme occasion?

If she will not shrink from this duty, she will ensure a victory beside which the ultimate conquest in this war will appear well-nigh insignificant.

X

WOMAN'S WAR WORK ON THE LAND

THE cry for woman's service on the land is one I endeavoured nearly twenty years ago to anticipate. It was at a time when the anxiety of girls to earn their own living was making itself manifest in every class, and when the wages paid to those who had broken away from the conventions of purely domestic life were miserably inadequate. I had heard how, in the Dominions overseas, English women had been forced to learn open-air duties as best they could, I had realised the natural instinct of many women for gardening, and I had no doubt that there would be some whose courage would not flinch from an experiment. Looking back to that season, I marvel at the progress feminism has wrought in the world. Then every development that was sought for men was in the case of woman taboo. The only thing that a girl might do in the garden without defying the conventions was the light job that could be accomplished without any fatigue. She might pluck roses; I have grave doubts as to whether she might plant or prune them.

85

She might eat celery, but the digging of a trench or the earthing-up of the plants would have been considered a most "unladylike" occupation. In fact, we suffered, as a sex, under the spell of that horrible word; life for women has not been nearly so futile since it was abolished.

In the years when I began first to find that the urgency of social problems was a bar to the further serenity of life, I, like other inexperienced people with reform at their hearts, dreamed dreams and saw visions. I had seen at Easton and Warwick the women of the working classes enjoying the hard work of the garden and the fields; I, too, had tried my hand, always to find that I was rewarded with a quickly renewed sense of the joy of life. Even when weather conditions were unfavourable, the rest after labour was in itself atonement for the toil—it was so unlike other rest. Then I began to see an England in which girls and young women, ceasing to be merely "ladylike," would be healthier, happier, and more useful than they had been in the years of which I could take count. I could not help realising that the desire for active physical exercise could not be limited to one sex, save in obedience to a convention that ignored human needs. It seemed to me as though the truth would be apparent to everybody, that nobody who could lend a helping hand would withhold it. Naturally I was soon undeceived.

I was assured that only the children of working farmers and labourers could possibly milk the dairy herd, that gardening work in many of its aspects would be beyond the limits of the capacity of the gently nurtured. The girl market gardener was voted an impossibility; as landscape gardener, I was assured, she could never compete with a man. Poultry-farming and stock-breeding were even voted indelicate! Household management, to enable girls to take posts as housekeepers in public institutions or large private houses, was regarded as something to be acquired without training, and even the commercial side of farm management was vetoed as a study for girls, as though a well-managed farm would be the worse for a competent book-keeper because that book-keeper chanced to be a daughter instead of a son of the house. I could prolong the list of vetoes and taboos that were presented to me, but no useful service would be served in doing so. I am only concerned to remember now—after nearly twenty years—that I was regarded as an unpractical dreamer, and that, as I write, there are letters on my desk asking me if I cannot recommend lady gardeners and agriculturists of all descriptions. I cannot: they are all fully occupied. Many are at work in England, not a few

are busy thousands of miles oversea—in Canada,
Australia, and the United States. Think of the
freedom and the fullness of their lives, never a taboo
to stand between them and any sane development!

To-day I see a great expansion of woman's labours under the sun. The trouble is that the demand outstrips the supply. The public, whose
apathy has given only a minimum of stimulus to
the progress of the girl agriculturist, has become
suddenly clamant. It demands the impossible. The
girls' agricultural colleges are to improvise the
highly trained, skilled article. It is as though they
should demand the finished fruits of the orchard
before the budding and flowering time of the trees
has been fulfilled. I am hoping that this will not
lead to a reaction, and that those whose demand for
ready-made service brings inevitably unsatisfactory
results will not regard woman's work in the light
that their own thoughtlessness must shed upon it.
Only those of us who understand the curriculum,
and the time required to follow it to the appointed
end, know that you must be thorough if you would
be successful. All the ordinary problems of the
open-air life must be faced in training before they
can be overcome in the practice of daily life in farm
and garden. To us this is a commonplace; to those
who do not know the land and its labor it comes as
a surprise and an annoyance.

I established the Hostel at Reading, near the great Agricultural College, in the year 1898, and it remained there for nearly four years, when the Reading premises began to prove inadequate to the purposes I had in view. Even when the ridicule ceased, the girls had not been popular at Reading, where the college students thought that they were intruders if they ventured beyond the dairy. There were certain advantages. For example, the heads of the house of Sutton opened their gardens at stated times, and the girls could see the most skilled work in operation. But I could not help thinking that, if the idea was to grow, it must have room and a congenial atmosphere for its development, and so it happened that the change was made. We moved to Studley Castle, in Warwickshire, sixteen miles from Birmingham, a rather modern place, with forty acres of gardens and pleasure grounds, wonderful out-buildings—built originally for racing stables—and nearly two hundred and fifty acres of farm land, with woodlands and water in addition. In many respects this was the ideal place for the work in hand. There are other institutions of similar kind in England to-day, and I am not claiming any special superiority for Studley. If I write of what is done there, it is merely because I know exactly what work is being carried on, and the full measure of success that attends it. Studley is now

run by a limited liability company, in which I have
no interest whatever. It differs from other agricultural colleges chiefly in the atmosphere, which is
that of Girton or Newnham, and is deliberately
preserved on grounds of economic policy.

If our victory in the world-war is to have in it
the elements of permanence, it can only be by the
thorough equipment of those who go out into the
world to contend with the most highly trained nation under the sun, and, as far as woman's education is concerned, in whatever aspect, it has the
advantage denied to the education of boys—of being free from old and paralysing conventions.
There is nothing that must be done merely because
it has been done from time immemorial, and the
agricultural colleges have been modern from their
inception.

The first thing to be considered is so to train the
students that they are able gradually to develop a
measure of physical strength, and at the same time
to teach them how to obtain a maximum of result
from a minimum of effort. Many an untrained man
could only accomplish with great exertion what a
trained woman can do without difficulty. In a
little while not only do the spade and the wheel-
barrow lose all their terrors, but the comparatively
light modern plough can be handled, even on fairly
heavy land, without excessive fatigue. Then the

balance must be preserved between practice and theory. You will remember that the method of combining the two is not new. Mr. Wackford Squeers taught it at Dotheboys Hall. "W-I-N-D-E-R, a casement. Now go and clean them." Perhaps this was the germ of the idea—who knows? The lecturer in the college is supplemented by the expert in the field, dairy, and garden, and the student is not limited to the grounds of the institution, ample though they be. On outlying farms, in private gardens, market gardens, at country flower shows and exhibitions, the pupils of this and other colleges are expected to demonstrate their efficiency, thereby learning how the familiar problems may vary in their incidents and application. There is no element of secrecy. All that is taught and all that is learned is open to the inspection of the section of the public that is interested. The college has terms similar to those of school and university —thirty-nine weeks of work and thirteen of holiday—and while girls are admitted as soon as their school education is finished, at the age of sixteen or thereabouts, women can join at any age. If they have the energy and determination, they are never too late to learn. For school-girls over twelve years of age who intend to take up agricultural or garden work when school days are over, there are holiday classes at which the 'prentice work may be studied under the most pleasant conditions possible. Most of the school-girls who take this course regard it as an ideal holiday.

For the benefit of adults who desire a special study, short courses can be arranged at all times, but it is, of course, well understood that such courses do not make the student truly representative of the college tuition. It has long been recognised that you cannot make agriculturists or horticulturists in a hurry. The minimum period of complete study is two years, but the complete course that turns out the finished student is a full three years. It is in view of this hard truth that I have eyed askance the suggestion that a course that is to be practical can be crowded into three months. Such a term would hardly avail a genius. As far as I have been able to see, the not very considerable percentage of failures associated with agricultural colleges is due to the inability of students to distinguish between enthusiasm and staying power. They have not realised that work must be done at every season and in nearly all weather, that the sun is not always shining, and that the novelty of association with Nature will wear away from all who are not Nature-lovers at heart and by instinct. That is why I am afraid of short-term training. Two or three years develop not only aptitude, but character; enthusiasms have

time to take a fresh and long lease of life. Training brings confidence too. Girls who wish to be
gardeners, agriculturists, poultry-farmers, estate
managers, and the rest, will do well to remember
that the new or the modern methods they are
taught in an up-to-date institution are not necessarily followed in the place where they get their
first engagement. If they have to control men,
they must expect to find a certain intolerance of
change, a certain resentment of direction. Unless
they are thoroughly sure of themselves they cannot supervise the work of others.

What the student has to remember is that most
of the methods she will find outside her training
college are wasteful, obsolete, or second rate. Sci-
entific training is unknown to the average gardener,
market gardener, dairy-farmer, and poultry-keeper.
Our old countryside is run on amasingly inept lines.
Foolishness of any kind that has behind it the sanction of a single generation is sacrosanct. If a father
has farmed or gardened foolishly, that special manner of foolishness is sacred to his son. We have
always relied upon "the foreigner." He sends us
fruit, eggs, honey, vegetables, corn, cattle food;
while the seas are open, we need never go hungry.
I do not pretend that we can do without him for
everything, but we can certainly do very much
more in the future than we have done in the past,

and we have been warned by our Government to do it. That is why I have so much hope for the future of the woman on the land. I feel that her work is no longer concerned with hobbies and private profit; henceforward it is, in effect, a kind of public service. The Government is avowedly anxious for the future of the land, frankly concerned to check the annual outlay of millions of pounds for foodstuffs that we are well able to raise at home.

Why, for example, should we spend forty thousand pounds a year upon honey, to name what our American friends would call "a side line," when we have a wealth of flowers and fruit blossom that would not only yield all that is required, but would even enable us to substitute honey for much of the sugar that is only sold to us when it has been chemically treated to improve appearance at the expense of quality? Why must we gather eggs from the far ends of the earth, and bacon from countries where pigs are fed as they are said to be fed in China? When I think of the thousands of women who are ready, willing, and, if properly trained, able to take a hand in the great task of feeding the people, it seems to me that the seed I sowed in 1898, to the accompaniment of much amusement, derision, and hostile criticism, has grown into a very sturdy and healthy tree. I even venture to think that the fruits will be more refresh-

ing than those of the Insurance Act itself. As far
as the records I have been able to examine teach
me, there have been very few failures to achieve
success among the women who have taken resolutely and completely to this comparatively new
walk in life. The students have done more than
merely earn a comfortable living. They have been
the disseminators of the new ideas, the modern
theories of agriculture, horticulture, and apiculture, the introducers of order and method into
realms where chaos ruled amiably and ineffectively.
In many cases they have even succeeded so far as
to disarm prejudice and to persuade omniscient man
that a method is not good merely because it is customary or easy to follow. And what they have done
is small by the side of what they may hope to do.

What is needed just now, when the Government
is really awake to the importance of woman's work
on the land, is an extension of the agricultural colleges and a series of State grants. At present the
work is costly. The upkeep of a big institution is
expensive, because you cannot treat the land precisely as you would for utility farming. It is there
to teach pupils, to carry out demonstrations. So
it is with the glass, that is so costly to build and
to heat. Then, again, professors—the best in the
country—must be asked to lecture; and while agricultural colleges are in the heart of the country,

the professors are probably living in distant university towns, so that their lectures are bound to be costly. Let us remember, too, quite frankly, that there is not much money for the girl who is not able to start a little establishment of her own or to go into partnership. There is a happy, healthy, useful life, there is valuable service, quite unrecorded, to the public at large, but the monetary reward is of the slightest and the training is long.

It is necessary, then, in view of the growing demand for the work of woman's hands, that the Government should make grants to the established colleges as they make grants to other educational bodies, and it would be well if every County Council that does not conduct an agricultural college of its own would give a few scholarships annually in the college nearest to its county town. These steps are needed to give an impetus to the work that is now being done. Had they been taken when first I pleaded for them, we should have been in quite a different position to-day. There would, at least, have been enough capable workers to meet the most pressing demands. At present they tell me that at Studley every post brings applications for gardeners and dairy workers, for women competent to train others, but there is not a single disengaged pupil. Doubtless a similar state of things obtains at the other colleges in Kent, Worcester-shire, Sussex, and elsewhere.

It has been seen that properly trained women can do all the work of farm and garden. Even ploughing is not beyond them, save on very stiff clay soils. They are entirely successful in handling animals; horses, cows, bullocks, sheep, pigs, and goats are all tractable when cared for by women. They are taught at all well-conducted institutions to substitute knack for force, and they have, as is admitted on all hands, the right temperament for tasks that demand not only time, but patience. As beekeepers they do very well, the gift of delicate handling standing them in good stead, and in the glasshouses they are easily first. Dr. Hamilton, the energetic and gifted Warden of Studley, tells me that she finds that the health of girls engaged upon the land, whether in the garden or on the farm, is good, and that many who arrive at the College in a delicate state of health grow very much stronger. She finds that the work makes women not only healthy, but happy—presumably because happiness is largely a product of good health.

Perhaps the needs of the country will be the de-termining factor in sending women to the land in the summer-times before us; but we may take it for granted that one of the results of war will be the large extension of the realm of the woman-worker of the field and garden. We cannot shut our eyes to the sad truth that there will be war widows in their thousands, and countless girls whose chances of married happiness have been destroyed. To many of these the land will supply the only anodyne that life has to offer. In hard work and the open air they will learn to forget; in the development of garden, or farm, or orchard they will find something to interest them. With their advent we may look to find a great addition to the national food supply, a great saving of money that has gone hitherto across the Channel or the Atlantic Ocean.

I am inclined to think that women are more likely than men to take advantage of the homeland opportunities. Men who have lived strenuously and dangerously may not be found content with a handful of acres and a cartload of restrictions at home, when the far-flung Dominions overseas have so much more with which to tempt them. I see that Sir Harry Verney's Committee, appointed to consider the question of land settlement for soldiers and sailors, suggested holdings of twenty-five acres for dairy-farming, and four-acre holdings for pigs, poultry, fruit, etc. These last are to cost £24 per annum. Consider as against this the one hundred and sixty acre grant of the Canadian Government, the additions made by the Canadian Pacific Railway and, perhaps, other great corporations, whereby a settler finds a house, farm buildings, fifty acres broken up and planted with wheat. There the rent is part payment of the purchase price. I do not think the Government is going to hold soldiers and sailors with anything Sir Harry Verney and his committee-men propose to offer, but I do think that if the Government will make a like offer to the women of England, and will arrange to do for them what it proposes to do for the men, this latest scheme of small holdings might well be a success. Women could and would make an agricultural colony. They delight in doing small things well; they are frugal and temperate; they can make much out of very little. Whatever their war experiences and suffering, it will not have developed in them the spirit of unrest. Their ambitions do not seek the particular kind of achievement that appeals most to men; they find happiness where a man might find boredom. They love the sense of independence, the freedom and simplicity that country life affords and enjoins.

Above all else that concerns woman's career on the land, it has clearly been shown now that in times of crisis the men who work on the land may be called away, and our home food supplies may be jeopardised by their absence. In these circumstances the movement must spread. The flower and market garden, the field, the conservatory, and the outhouse must be recognised as providing a pleasant sphere of activity for girls and women, and there is more than enough land in these islands to provide small holdings for many years to come for all who have the will and the capacity to develop them. In conclusion, let me utter a warning that demands the attention of all who love their country. At the present time we only produce about twenty per cent. of the food we eat. For the rest we depend upon our mercantile marine and our power to hold, not only the seas, but the skies above and the depths beneath. Without any comment, it seems to me that this simple and undeniable statement should suffice to settle the career of many a sturdy country-loving English girl.

XI

GERMAN WOMEN AND MILITARISM

READING the record of Germany's war methods, even those of us who are endeavouring to think sanely through these evil days must be impressed by the overwhelming evidence of their complete ruthlessness.

We who have travelled in Germany not once, but many times, know full well that harshness and cruelty are not associated with the majority. There are countless Germans who could only be cruel in obedience to orders, and, of course, every German will do what he is told, just as the Children of Israel did when Joshua, who appears to have invented "frightfulness," was carrying out his merciless campaign. If we admit that the simple German of the south is not cruel at heart, that he is rather a dreamer and a sentimentalist with strong love for domestic pleasures, we find that the policy of "frightfulness" must be ascribed to the military party, consisting for the most part of Prussians, with headquarters in Berlin.

These men are the organisers of war, and speak

through the mouths of writers like Treitschke, Bernhardi, and the rest. It is they who have torn up the treaties and conventions that were, humanity hoped, to decide the conduct of war. They are responsible for the curious outburst of national hatred against this country that is at once so startling and so silly, a revelation of the sad truth that Germany is suffering from neurosis.

I have been trying to trace "frightfulness" to its source, not through the medium of books or papers, but in the light of my own knowledge of the country and my past acquaintance with some of its leading men, and I think that the philosophic historian of the times to come, whose vision is not obscured by the smoke of battle or the fury of combatants, will not hesitate to declare that the worst and saddest features of war as waged by the Germans are due to the fact that in their country women are kept more in the background than in the country of any other great Power.

The fault, as I will point out later on, is not that of the women, but of the leaders of German faction who have deliberately suppressed woman, and of nearly all the leaders of German thought who, being dependent on Government favour, have subscribed to their policy of deliberate suppression. Here and there an independent thinker has arisen nearly always from the ranks of Social Democracy.

Bebel's book on women, for example, is a standard work, but the few lights do no more than emphasise the surrounding darkness.

Look round Europe for a moment. Russia is a backward empire and the spirit of progress moves over it with slow feet, but Russia is making vast strides, and the plough that will trace deep furrows in the virgin soil of its social life is drawn by man and woman together. All the professions are open to women, even those in which women are not found here. The Russian engineer who planned the newest bridge over the Neva was a woman. Men and women students work side by side on terms of absolute equality, and compete for honours that often fall to the gentler sex.

Russian women of the educated classes are more than merely well informed, they are brilliant. Linguists, women of affairs, they have a grip of actualities of the empire of which they form a significant part. In spite of autocratic rule and limited freedom there is such a full life for the Russian woman as her German sister has never known, except in dreams of emancipation. In Finland, be it remembered, women sit in Parliament.

Turn to France, and it may be declared emphatically that woman rules. Women are doctors, barristers, and scientists; they are members of the Goncourt Academy; they are the heads of some of the most important business institutions; they give the most exclusive *salons* their distinction. Public opinion is moulded by them; their influence makes and breaks Cabinets. Feminism is one of the strongest forces in France. Quiescent to-day or working in quietness, this force will dominate a France released from war.

Even in Belgium, of whose progress we hear little, women have been largely responsible for the organisation of the middle and working classes, an organisation that was well-nigh complete before war broke out, and in the slow rebuilding that is to come we may look with confidence to the Belgian woman to play a leading *rôle*. Turn to a group of neutral countries—Denmark, Norway, Sweden—and it will be seen that feminism is moving with vast strides along the path of national progress. Woman is asserting herself in all of them, contributing her thought to her country's problems, taking an ever important place in its councils.

Alone of the great Powers Germany has elected to forget or to disregard as a negligible quantity the opinion of woman, and the reason is not far to seek. For years past the German has forgotten the respect and reverence he owes to his own womenfolk. *Kuche, Kinder, Kirche*—he calls alliteration to his aid to express a growing contempt for the sex and the narrowest possible view of its world function. Intoxicated with the vision of imperial domination, he has regarded his own sex as the one motive force in the universe.

He has not watched the slow awakening of women in the countries around him; he has not noted how bonds of sympathy, light as gossamer, yet strong as steel, have stretched from country to country, binding our sex in a large and ever widening sisterhood, inarticulate now, or at least hardly coherent, but only waiting for their appointed hour to assume a fuller share of the glories, the burdens and the responsibilities of life. Woman's influence, silent, world-wide, pervasive, has been treated by the evangels of Kultur as though it were nonexistent, and in the hour of crisis woman as a united force has avenged herself for years of neglect, scorn and brutality. She is everywhere a belligerent.

I do not know the country in Europe where women are treated as they are in Germany. Not many countries can vie with the United States in the attention bestowed upon the gentler sex, but as I have endeavoured to show, they are respected more in every belligerent country than they are in the one that sought to rest supreme in Europe. Even in Italy, Spain, and Portugal, where women must often work as hard as men, they stand upon a secure footing of affection and respect. The

smaller courtesies, the greater services of life are
theirs. In some definite measure they complete
the home. But you cannot bring an indictment
against a whole nation, and I do not seek to do so.

In tens of thousands of German homes the wife
and daughters are loved and honoured, but in the
rank and file of military circles, even among the
men who hold official positions and boast a certain
standing, woman has been dethroned—she is regarded as an incumbrance necessary for the production of further generations of supermen, who shall
inherit the earth. This attitude of mind reveals
itself in the action that speaks louder than words.
The toleration and the contempt to which I refer
are everywhere apparent. No good-looking woman
is safe in Germany from the ill-bred stares and
comments of the men with whom she must travel
in train or tram.

If women enter a theatre or restaurant their
own friends and relatives do not rise to receive
them. They are liable to be elbowed into the road
if men walking abreast can occupy the whole of
the pavement. The politeness of the few cultured
Germans (pardon the discredited adjective) merely
emphasises the boorishness of the vast majority. It
might be that the German is waiting for women
to be officially recognised as human beings to whom
some measure of courtesy or even decency is due.

Only when rudeness is *"verboten"* will rudeness cease.

The country is governed by men for men and women, but according to the marriage rubric woman is actually man's servant. The effect of these conditions upon the morals of the country is deplorable. They give a cachet to vices, even the most odious, and the rate of illegitimacy, about 10 per cent. for the whole empire, is about doubled in Berlin, where the military caste is supreme. The morals of the army are the morals of Berlin, and account not only for the hideous stories published about what took place in Belgium and northern France, but for the recitals not less appalling that one gathers from officers home on leave who have seen sights in the area of German occupation that cannot be set down in print.

Undoubtedly these recitals, if they could reach the heart of Germany, would thrill tens of thousands of honest men with indignation and disgust. I do not believe for a moment that they represent the inclinations of the whole nation. They are rather the action of that section of the nation which, while war endures, must have the upper hand, and during all the years of war-like preparations has reigned supreme. Against this aspect of German national life the women of belligerent and neutral countries alike are arrayed. Whatever their re-

sources or their influence in the councils of their
husbands, sons, and brothers, it will be devoted without cease to the destruction of a militarism that
degrades and shames womankind. The German
woman knows in her heart that her men have in
countless instances become perverts, but she is
dumb because she is forbidden to speak. In Prussia no woman may organise a union that has political aims; she may not even join one.

It is the purpose of the dominant caste to keep
woman in subjection, to restrict her activities to
the kitchen, the cradle and the Church, even to deny
her the mental and the physical development that
might tend to lead her to revolt. Woman may
find a limited salvation in the conduct of a business; throughout the German Empire not far short
of a million women conduct commercial enterprises
of one kind or another, and collectively they strive
with some success to better the physical and moral
conditions under which their sisters live. No effort of which they have yet been capable has accomplished more than this, their condition of tute-
lage remains complete.

I do not pretend to be satisfied with the position of women in England: far from it; but here,
as in the countries already enumerated, it is better far than in Germany. Women mould public
opinion to an appreciable extent; they are able

to modify the life of their sex in many important particulars, the best of them exercise sane influence, and all are sufficiently well treated to establish a definite attitude of mind in men. We know that no British or French troops would behave in Germany as Germans behaved in Belgium; we know that the honour of honourable women and of helpless children would be safe in the keeping of the French and British officer, and that he would not be called upon to restrain his men from acts of lust and savagery.

We know that there is a public opinion the wide world over among free women and women struggling to be free that will not submit to the domination of any race that does not hold woman in respect. It is on this account, in my opinion, that the unbridled and tolerated savagery of the worst class of German conscript in Belgium and France has cost Germany more than the loss of half a dozen pitched battles. Whatever the irritation caused by the incidents of the war, the Allies know that women the world over are and will remain on their side, for the hegemony of a nation that treats women in peace with contempt and in war with "frightfulness" cannot be contemplated by our sex. We know that in fighting for the cause of the Allies we are fighting for the most downtrodden of the highly civilised women in Europe. At present they would resent our aid—they are patriotic —they have suffered terribly, and in the hour of their trials they mourn and forgive those who treated them ill.

Later on, when peace returns, when the world is purged of violence and its wounds begin their slow and painful process of healing, the German women will recognise that we have been fighting for a larger cause than our own; that we helped to force the doors that have remained barred so long and to break the chains that bound the women of a great but erring nation. Only the ultimate triumph of the Allies can free the women of Germany, and in time they will realise the truth.

The views of the wisest men are narrow, and few among them will realise or admit even now the truth that woman is now a factor in the world's affairs. When this war is over we shall tell in no uncertain words what is in our hearts. At present we must needs be silent. If those dreamers of world empire had but remembered that women, too, have minds and are learning to use them, the story of the great world tragedy, even if it had to be set down, would have been widely different in many of its incidents.

It was Germany's fatal mistake that, not content with dominating its own womankind and suppressing them whenever and wherever possible, it believed that the rest of the world was equally indifferent to the treatment of its mothers, wives, and daughters.

Every known outrage has raised fresh fighters, has strengthened the Allies with the sure force of moral sympathy and encouragement, has thinned the ranks of those whose sympathies were with a country whose marvellous progress provides so much material for admiration. Who can measure the responsibility of those guides and teachers who taught the German to develop along material lines and to forget that woman is the proper spiritual guide, and that as man loves and reverences her he sees farther and deeper into the heart of things —sees life sanely and sees it whole?

Whatever the limitations of our knowledge we know that the one sex completes the other; that man enlarges the vision of woman and woman enlarges the vision of man, and that it is the peculiar gift of our sex to control man's passions, to stimulate his humanity, to direct his ambitions away from dangerous paths. We do not all strive as we might; we do not always succeed as we deserve, but man is woefully incomplete without us, and the spectacle of a nation that has despised womanhood waging war shows that this contempt corrodes his moral fibre, leaves him at the mercy of his worst instincts and raises up against him

all the spiritual forces against which none may
strive victoriously.

We women who have never handled weapons,
whose only place in the area of strife is among the
maimed and helpless, know even better than men
that the race is not always to the swift nor the
battle to the strong. When history has recorded
the story of the world war that darkens our lives
to-day, future generations will ask how it was
that Germany could find no friends among the
neutral nations. Her Ambassadors, official and
unofficial, her publicists and those of neutral countries who were not ashamed to accept her subsidies,
worked with true German thoroughness. Truth
was never allowed to stand in the way of propaganda. No lie that might serve a useful purpose
went unsanctioned, for the great end was to sanctify all means, however vile, and yet in the hour
when even moral support and silent sympathy
would have been of the greatest value, Germany
looked for it in vain.

It was easy to declare that the whole world was
jealous and misinformed; such an excuse could
hardly deceive the responsible people who fathered
it. My own view is that the women of Europe
and the United States turned against Germany
when the manner in which she waged war was first
revealed to a disgusted world. Their hostility was

not merely sentimental—it was psychological. The German attitude toward women, already questioned, was revealed as in the glare of searchlight, and womanhood from London to Petrograd and from Copenhagen to New York was completely, irrevocably antagonised.

XII

YOUTH IN THE SHAMBLES

IT becomes increasingly difficult to speak one's mind in England to-day, even though one has no peace scheme to propound and no efficient public servant to criticise.

Liberty has vacated her throne, or as much of it as Privilege would ever allow her to occupy, and the Defence of the Realm Act has taken her place.

Consequently it is very hard to express opinions unless they are sufficiently platitudinous to gain universal and immediate acceptance. Roughly speaking we are all of one mind about the conduct of this war; the minority in opposition is so small that it can be disregarded, but we are all at variance as to method, and on the Ship of State that steers such an erratic course through the hurricane of strife there is hardly a passenger who is not convinced that he could reach the goal much more rapidly than the man at the wheel is likely to.

Those who criticise the steering are suspect, for the national temper is a little upset, our situation

is without precedent, and an Englishman dislikes
novelty. ˙I cannot help my belief that it is the novelty rather than the tragedy of the hour that
troubles him most. He is giving, to the best of his
capacity, blood, labour, treasure, but he is not
thinking as deeply as he should, perhaps because
he understands that when you begin to think and
believe you see a great truth clearly, you are
morally bound to communicate that truth to others.
Then the Defence of the Realm comes in and you
are likely to be hailed a traitor to all good causes
by the first person who—with or without understanding your views—disagrees with them!

Yet for all the prejudices with which the expression of opinion is beset, it is hard to keep silent
when something presents itself to the mind in the
guise of a vital truth, and now, after more than
two years of war have forced reflection and taught
us to see the world tragedy as a whole, there are
things that must needs be said, protests that must
needs be made.

Of all the iniquities that are associated with war,
war as distinct from murder I would add, there
is nothing quite so horrible as the sacrifice of young
life. It is common to all the nations at war. We
read of boys of fifteen fighting in the ranks of our
enemies, and, at home, of boys who have added a
year or two to their proper age to deceive a not

too inquisitive recruiting sergeant.   To raw lads
in their utter ignorance, war is a great joy and
adventure; they are proud to help their country
and to be redeemed from the charge of being "slack-
ers."   So when the cup of life is hardly at their
lips they go, some to die, some to be maimed, some
to return prematurely old and broken down.

While the plots and counter plots that made for
war were being hatched, these young warriors were
in the nursery, or at school.   Even now they have
reached no perception of the real forces for which
men strive; until war broke out their lives were still
supposed to be under the protection of their
parents.

But as soon as the State is beset it calls for aid,
not alone upon matured men, who understand and
have a sense of responsibility, but upon the lads
whom it ought to be protecting as the one irre-
placeable asset of the next generation.

Wise old gentlemen with a very tolerable imi-
tation of the spirit of prophecy in their hearts, pens
in their hands, and bees in their bonnets, wrote indignant articles in the best read organs of the press
that our downfall, if we did not introduce conscription, is merely a matter of months.   Sometimes it
was weeks.   The time given to us varied according to the measure of the writers' chronic dyspepsia.

Yet if these people would only think, they would

have little difficulty in admitting that the lads who
have been well educated, well trained and prepared with infinite labour for life are just those who
should not be surrendered to death under any normal conditions until they have fulfilled their primary function toward the State.

I will go farther and suggest that their elders
have no right to rob them of the few years in
which they taste the joys of life. I was told recently by a man who knew what he was talking
about that under the Mosaic Code the Jews did not
allow their married men to go to war until they
had spent one year with their wives. A man who
was betrothed was instructed to marry, and even
if a man married a second time he had to remain
for one year at home. In this way the continuity
of the race was assured and the Jews, eminently
a fighting nation, preserved their virility.

There was no question of sentiment involved—
it was hard, common sense applied to war. And,
horrible irony, the British Government recognises
the simple truth, but has only learned down to
the present to apply it to farm stock. I saw last
year a printed notice in the country post-offices
issued to farmers by the Board of Agriculture, telling them not to kill lamb and veal because whatever the price offered the removal of immature

stock is dangerous wastefulness which the country cannot afford.

Here is a copy of the notice:

BOARD OF AGRICULTURE AND FISHERIES

———

SPECIAL NOTICE TO FARMERS

———

PRESERVE OUR FLOCKS AND HERDS!
MAINTAIN OUR MEAT SUPPLY!

———

The Board of Agriculture and Fisheries strongly urge all Farmers to RAISE AS MUCH STOCK AS POSSIBLE during the war.

Their advice to you is:

Do NOT send breeding and immature stock to the BUTCHER simply because prices are attractive now.

Do NOT MARKET half-finished animals; it is wasteful of the country's resources and is against your own interests.

Do NOT KILL CALVES—rear them; it is well worth it.

Do NOT REDUCE your stock; when you cannot buy stores, buy calves.

MAINTAIN your flocks and breed your sows; it will pay you to do so.

The Board of Agriculture and Fisheries make the above recommendations not only for the NATIONAL WELFARE but because they believe them to be for the ultimate benefit of BRITISH AGRICULTURE.

It seems almost too ridiculous to be true that the Government has more concern for lambs or calves than for boys on the threshold of manhood, but the facts convict them.

For myself I would rather see a thousand of the bloodthirsty old gentlemen who preached conscription sent to the front from their club smoke-rooms and editorial chairs, than five hundred lads from whom their country has something to expect!

I do not think I am a sentimentalist, certainly I do not plead for the exemption of mere boys from the battlefield in order that they may have what is called a good time, though I hold that they should not be deprived deliberately of the few halcyon years that are in one fashion or another the reward of one and all. I would work them to the last ounce of their capacity in seasons like these. They should have long hours, Spartan fare, and spells of physical drill, they should put in eight hours of labour for the Government in the factory, in the munition works, wherever their services could be best employed.

They might be under military rule, amenable to the same discipline as the soldier, but they should not go into the firing line, because they belong to the next generation.

They are to sire it; no nation can afford to leave that responsibility to the physically unfit, and to those who have passed fighting age.

This duty done, they would be free to join the

fighting forces for which their drill, their labour
and their self-denial would have prepared them.
My soldier relatives and friends tell me that the
lad in his teens is of little value in a prolonged campaign. He may have all the necessary courage, but
he lacks the essential stamina. He is fitter to march
and endure when he is twenty-five than when he is
nineteen, fitter still at thirty.

But, asks my critic, where will you recruit your
fighting men? I look round at my men friends,
and I find them, up to the age of fifty, taking their
chance in the forefront of things. The outcry
against the married man as combatant is valid only
in so far as his family depends upon him for support. My friends chance for the greater part to
belong to the comfortable classes. They have enjoyed the best that England has to offer; they are
prepared to pay the price, with their lives if need
be. Above all they are articulate, they have the
franchise, they can speak their mind. Collectively
they support in one form and another the conditions that make war possible. They are conscious
of a certain responsibility.

Where, for example, on the other hand, is the
responsibility of the midshipman on the torpedoed
battleship? I take his bravery for granted. I am
quite convinced that could he read my plea he would
disavow any shadow of sympathy with it, but I am

concerned for the country and not for him. He
has a duty toward civilisation, he is well-bred,
highly trained, efficient. I say that the State owes
him at least a few years of manhood and should
see that he is allowed to reach maturity, although
he is neither veal nor lamb!

It is false economy that raises the outcry against
married men as soldiers. They alone in the community can be spared, they have fulfilled, or partly
fulfilled, the function upon which civilisation depends. Potentially, if not always actually, they are
fathers. Economists insist that pensions and al-
lowances are an extravagance that the nation cannot
afford. I reply that war is a still greater extravagance, the wickedest form of indulgence known to
mankind, and that worse than war is the destruction of the fairest hopes of the future, the race to
come. Again, if those who light the fire were compelled to feed the flames I believe there would be
fewer conflagrations.

I feel that I do but set down facts that are known
to thinkers, who, as a rule, prefer to keep silence
at times like these lest their patriotism be suspect.
After the war they will deplore the ruin; trustees
for the generation to come, they will see that they
have failed in their trust. They will shift the responsibility on to the nature of things, they will
declare that war was inevitable and that destruction

of all we hold most dear must follow in its wake.

Here I join issue with them. The world is for all practical purposes ruled by mankind. Nothing but the catastrophes like the tidal wave and the earthquake escape man's control. Famine, disease, and mortality he can arrest; he can increase his stature morally, mentally, physically. If he elect to play the prodigal he does so at his own risk, but he has no right to tamper with the vital resources of the generations that must follow. War is delirium, or he would bear this fundamental truth in mind. I think it has escaped him. He is immersed in the pursuit of the end, and no means are spared. Thus we hear the outcries because the fat money bags are growing thin, but nothing is said of the great asset that no trading, however successful, can restore.

We can find in some barbarous land wealth only comparable to that which Sindbad discovered in the Valley of Diamonds, but what will that profit a race that must depend upon old and exhausted stock to renew its vitality? The desire for wealth is at least one of the contributory causes of war, the thought of wealth wasted makes men forget they are wasting what no wealth can replace.

I am sure that women feel this eternal truth in their hearts, but all too many fear to be thought afraid. They fear their own mankind, those for whom they would gladly sacrifice all that life holds for them of good. They fear to be thought jealous for their own boys, while if the truth be told their fear is all for the young sons of all women quite irrespective of nationality. At least this is how the situation appeals to me, and I dare not keep silent if there be any medium of appeal to those who think with me that will set my thoughts down. There is a slumbering conscience of humanity only waiting the call that will break through its dreams. I am not so bold as to believe that I can utter it, but I may perchance stimulate some more gifted pen.

In any case, I cannot hide my thoughts merely because they may meet no response, for after all there is not in all the world a single great belief that was not once the unregarded possession of a single mind.

XIII

THOUGHTS ON COMPULSION

WHILE I am firmly opposed to conscription in any form that does not embrace national wealth and resources as well as men, or that singles out one class of men to the exclusion of others, while I believe that, even subject to this view of national obligation, conscription should be treated as a war measure and blotted out of the statute book in the month that sees the restoration of peace, I am not writing to protest or to complain. We are told that every cloud has its silver lining, and when the Government decided to demand the services of those unmarried men who, far more by reason of apathy than cowardice, had remained to be taken, I could not help thinking that much good might come of it. Against the hideous doctrine that the end justifies the means we may set the equally old saying that necessity knows no law, and against the compulsory making of soldiers which is an evil, I set the waking of the national consciousness, and that is a gain.

For centuries England led the vanguard of the

workers for freedom. Against the will of the people the power of the great barons and of their Kings bent and broke. There were generations in which the people as a people were articulate, they stood up for their rights and privileges and were a force that few dared defy. The discovery of steam, the growth of factories, the increase of population and the struggle for life combined to make a large section of the working classes helpless. The hideous poverty and ugliness of life in the great centres of wealth drove men, and women too, to shut out the ugliness of their lives with the aid of brief spells of dissipation. Strong drink became alike a source of revenue to the country, a source of "honours"— generally paid for in hard cash—to the prosperous brewer and distiller, and the source of brief forgetfulness, misery, disease, crime and savage punishment to those who sought its dangerous solace. National expenditure and party funds alike clamoured for the maintenance of the evil, and those who are most concerned with what is euphemistically called "keeping the working classes in their places" turned a deaf ear to schemes that sought to make the places of leisure for the worker more attractive and less dangerous. Pure Beer Bills and legislation to restrict the sale of spirits to such spirit as is matured, met with no effective support. Give the worker the nineteenth and twentieth century substitutes for his old time *panem et circenses* and he would continue until strength failed him to sow that others might reap and to earn the opprobrium and contempt of those he enriched.

Parliament, immersed in politics to the exclusion of government, cared little for the real welfare of the people. It contrived by skilful electioneering to stimulate their interests in things that do not matter, and when they were not wanted at the polls their representatives—save the mark—left them severely alone. So it happened, as time passed, that the old interest in vital questions was passing from a large section of the proletariat. Powerful through the medium of their Unions they supported these great organisations for little better than the right to live. It was so hard to improve the conditions of a trade or a group of allied industries that the effort to this end left them with no energies to enter into larger fields. Those leaders of the people who have the gift of clear vision could meet with no adequate response, they alone could see the wood, their followers had their gaze riveted on one particular tree. England tended more and more to become the paradise of the capitalist and the purgatory of the working man, and because he was always protesting against conditions that will fill future generations with wonder and shame, conditions improved beyond recognition by the country with which we are now engaged in a life-and-death struggle, it became the practice of the comfortable classes to denounce the workman and all his ambitions. He was, in their view, sent into this world to create wealth, not to enjoy what it creates; that was the privilege of his betters. The Englishman's natural sense of fair play has been obscured by the newspapers that pander to him and give him all his thoughts ready made; if anybody thinks this is an extreme statement, let him turn to the files of the reactionary press from the time when John Burns led the Dockers' Strike down to the outbreak of war (and since) and see whether he can find anywhere a solitary favourable verdict for the worker as against the employer. He will search in vain.

There is a certain psychological aspect of the labour question that has, I think, been overlooked. A generation or two of oppressive conditions tends to produce a race that loses national consciousness. The worker learns to take the view that he is no longer a part of Great Britain, that his interests are exclusively personal, like those of his employers, that he has no status in the country and that his business is to get the most tolerable conditions of life that he can secure by combination and agitation, and to ignore the trend of politics, religion, social progress, and the rest of the life forces of civilisation. He knows himself for one who hews wood and draws water, it suffices him to carry a minimum of logs to the pile and buckets from the spring. He knows that there is for him no glimpse of the larger life and that because he is collectively a multitude there will be keen competition to batten on his small savings or surpluses. He has the feeling that if he loses his job he will take his place in the ranks of a submerged tenth, ranks easy to slip into, almost impossible to rise from. My long intercourse with those who fast that others may feast has revealed this attitude to me in a hundred shapes, all tragic, some dangerous. It has been the despair of those who are working for the people and know that if they would but combine to grasp the sorry state of things environing them they could "shatter it to pieces and remould it nearer to the heart's desire." Unhappily it is impossible to fight what is called *vis inertiæ*, you cannot bruise a feather pillow or hurt a sack of sand by striking it, and while long hours, scanty holidays, mean pleasures and continual anxiety dogged the footsteps of the working classes, it seemed impossible to secure the unity of action, the collective wisdom that would not only enable labour to find its place in the sun, but would destroy the parasites that thrive upon it. I think that the careful observer who noted the social condition of England down to the late summer of 1914 will be disposed to agree that I have not overstated the case or put the ugly lighting unfairly on the foreground of the picture.

Then came war with its strange, unmistakable revelation to the working man and working woman. In the blinding light born of battle they saw their country assaulted by an enemy completely trained and organised. Women saw that their own rulers had been too immersed in the great games of party politics and business development to give proper thought for the safety of the country. They saw, too, that the limitations of capitalism and capitalist were visible in the eyes of the world. They could help, they could leaven the dough of profit-making with the yeast of personal sacrifice, some have done so, but for the salvation of the country they appealed to the working man. Government adopted some of his own panaceas, they accepted schemes of pure socialism as props for the pillars of the State, they taxed riches and laid sacrilegious hands upon the Dagon of wealth to the infinite rage of certain Philistines who are still grieving for the god's lost hands and feet, but it was to the working classes Government turned in the hour of their distress, and Labour responded nobly. Those into whose souls the iron of corruption, disappointment and indifference had not entered, set themselves to labour seven days a week for long hours in evil at-

mosphere, or left their sweethearts and wives to
strike a blow for the country that had displayed
to them more of the qualities of a step-mother than
a mother. Many have laid down their lives, and
in the hearts of those who survive national consciousness has been re-born.

The democratic comradeship of the battlefield,
embracing all classes, has taught the working man
that his foe in times of peace is not so much the
class whose representatives are of his own blood
brotherhood, but the system that dominates those
who serve and those who accept service. This lesson learned exclusively on the fields of war will
permeate the factories when war is over. One
stumbling-block to progress remained. It was, I
venture to say, the presence in our midst of hundreds of thousands of men who have been rendered
listless and apathetic by life conditions too easy
or too hard. Now compulsion has reached this
class it will give them in return for unsought risks
and labour a sense of their place in the body politic.
It will teach them that whether they will or no
they have a part to play in shaping the destinies
of Great Britain and that the reward will be in
proportion to the sacrifice. We must not forget
that a new Britain, a new Empire, a new Imperial
outlook is being shaped over the far-flung area of
war. It will not be only to the British Empire

that change will come, but to all belligerent nations. The upheaval, sure as the succession of day and night, is one we dare hardly comtemplate, not by reason of fear, but by reason of hope. To take advantage of the change as it will affect our nation, all classes of the community must prepare, and nothing could have clogged the wheels of progress in the near future than the presence in our midst of so many thousands of men whose inactivity would have been bitterly resented by those who have borne the heat and burden of the day. Unity of action is a condition precedent to the close and merciless revision of existing conditions, the ending of privilege, the widening of the powers of democracy, the whole peaceful solution of a question that two years ago promised to develop into a war worse than this we are waging, a war of brother against brother.

I repeat that I am opposed to conscription, particularly to a conscription that picks and chooses, and does not demand capital as freely as it demands life; equally am I opposed to the action of the young and unattached men who shrink from assuming their proper responsibilities. That they would have held back if the conditions of their life, whether favourable or unfavourable, had been the true conditions of an enlightened citizenship, I sincerely doubt, that they should have been forced to undertake as a duty what they should have embraced as a privilege is matter for regret. Happily they will not go unrewarded, they will see their errors, and they will come back to a country they have helped to save with the keenest determination to make it worth living in as well as worth fighting for.

XIV.

"WHY is it," wrote an editor, criticising a view of women that I had put forward, "why is it that woman is actually a war lover at heart, an inciter to and encourager of war? Can you explain why, while some women condemn fighting, the great majority do not shrink from it, and even regard the fighting man as the proper object of their admiration?" It was a challenge, that I will answer to the best of my ability.

In the first place, I must admit that the statement is true about countless women. Only yesterday I had a letter from a friend to whom I had written my sympathy; her only son was killed in the British advance. "I need no more consolation," she wrote. "Harry's colonel has sent me a letter telling me of my poor boy's bravery. I am proud to think that he has lived up to our tradition—ours has always been a fighting family, you know."

I would not criticise a bereaved mother; I can never forget that my eldest son has been in the fighting line, that my other boy gave up Cambridge

133

for the aviation school, and is now flying in France, that my son-in-law is a soldier, and that of many friends and a few relatives only the memory remains. But I feel, from the bottom of my heart, that the death and glory idea is wrong; that the attraction of medals, ribbons, stars, orders, titles and uniforms and brass buttons is false, and that an ever-increasing number of women are conscious of the truth, not only here but in France, Germany, Austria, Russia and Italy.

That consciousness cannot become fully articulate until the war is over. For each belligerent nation the duty at this moment is clear—it must fight for what it holds to be right, must struggle for victory until the end. When that end comes I believe that the reign of the old ideas will end with it, and that all women will recognise the truth that is already clear as daylight to the minority.

Why is woman actually a war lover at heart? The question stings me. I am almost reluctant to answer. Yet though the fault is woman's, the responsibility is man's. Down to only a few years ago woman was no more than man's toy. She existed for his pleasure and convenience. If he covered her with pretty dresses and radiant jewels it was because she was his chattel. It seems only yesterday that a married woman's property became her husband's when he married her; that she could

not bring an action at law. It needed the cele-
brated Jackson case, familiar to students of the
feminist movement, to decide that a man might
not lock his wife up in his house.

I believe that the law enabling a man to administer "moderate chastisement" to his wife has
never been repealed. A woman cannot divorce her
drunken, dissolute husband unless he ill-uses her
physically; the law, unable to deny that woman
has a body, will not grant her the possession of
a soul. Trashy novels, trivial amusement, unending decoration, freedom from the development of
mentality and personality—these are the things that
have been held to suffice women, and though there
have always been a few great women in the world,
the vast majority has been compelled to accept the
conditions offered.

I cannot help thinking that if there had not
been a surplus of women over men in countries
where monogamy rules, change would have been
longer still in coming; but there have always been
tens of thousands of women for whom there is
neither mate, domestic inactivity nor child-bearing,
and the educational progress, though leaden footed,
has moved.

From the Garden of Eden to Ibsen's "Dolls'
House" is a far cry, but it was left to the great
Scandinavian dramatist to open woman's eyes.

That is, I think, why he was greeted by male critics with such howls of execration—they saw the foundation of the old order being sapped. Man had appealed to woman's vanity, and had consequently developed it enormously; but the motive was little higher than that which inspires the male baboon when he goes courting. Ibsen showed woman the result of her submission.

Only the historian, looking at our social history when the youngest of us "has lain for a century dead," will realise the strength and progress of the feminist movement in the last decade or two; the barriers it has surmounted or swept away; the barbed wire entanglements of prejudice and convention against which it has flung itself. Yet I am bold enough to declare that had universal war been mooted in 1934 instead of 1914 woman throughout all the countries of potential combatants would have combined instantly to prevent it.

At present the ranks of the thinkers are too thin; woman is divided against herself. The worst foes of feminism are women; it is the anti-feminists who parade the streets in khaki, who band themselves into wholly unnecessary and sometimes disreputable anti-German leagues, who labour as though war were a glory rather than a curse. You will not find militarists or anti-feminists among the glorious sisterhood of the hospitals, for they

almost alone among women know what war really
is. If the propaganda of feminism could have
spread, if it could have invaded Germany, where
the Church, the nursery and the kitchen are expected to fill every woman's life, what a very different answer would have been given to the ambitions of rulers and the blundering of politicians!
In how many million homes, where sadness reigns
supreme, would there have been the simple, harmless happiness that is the birthright of us all?

Is it the irony of fate that man must pay the
terrible price for having made woman what she is;
for having stifled or sought to stifle her common
sense; for robbing her of the rights that she pos-
sesses by reason of being a human being; for dis-
tracting her with gawds and frivolities, and seeking
to keep her merely as a minister to his pleasures and
a mother to his children? He has paid for the
supreme folly of generations with the price of the
lives of millions of his best and bravest, with the
ruin of flourishing cities and fair country, with
the poverty of the generation to come, and with
many another bitter offering of which he is not
yet fully aware.

Doubtless there are still in our midst countless
women who accept all that is happening as inevitable; who look upon it without realising that had
the sex responded to the ideals of feminism and

become one sisterhood without boundaries and
without a limited patriotism conditioned by the ac-
cident of birth, these things could not have been.
I say, without hesitation, that the future of the
world demands the elimination of some existing
types of women, the education of others, and, in
the end, the union of all.

Man was not born merely for glorious death,
he was born for glorious life, and in the systematic
and universally condoned slaughter of man by man
there is neither honour nor glory. The world, properly administered, can produce enough food and
clothing for all; it has work and a measure of happiness for all. Our enemies are not Englishmen
or Germans, Frenchmen or Turks; they are ignorance and poverty, disease and vice. Woman recognises the truth—that is to say, thinking and eman-
cipated woman recognises it—and she knows that
all the strife that tears the older world asunder
is fratricidal, that a million times Cain strikes down
a million times Abel, and in so doing deliberately
obscures the Divine Event toward which all creation
moves.

Woman falters, she is young in mental growth
and still very weak, though growing stronger hour
by hour. She sees nothing of war, but she hears
of moving incidents by flood and field and hairbreadth 'scapes in the imminent deadly breach, and

her sense of romance so largely fostered by pernicious or trivial literature is stirred to its depths. She wants for her son or her husband or her lover some of the dust of praise, some of the ribbons and medals, some of the glory in which she will discern some pale reflection of herself.

She falls in love with war because she has not the least inkling of its realities; her mourning garments are edged with pride. It has been left to this terrible struggle to tear some of the bandages from her eyes and to rob her of an unworthy ideal. What a supreme misfortune that world tragedy has supervened while she is growing up, before she has learned to grasp the power that lies to hand! In instances beyond numbering she has passed the feminist movement by, quite content to hug her chains as long as they are heavily gilded. She does not realise and does not believe in her own powers, and in Central Europe, at least, she has been kept under surveillance all the time.

England, France, and America are the great Powers that have given feminism a chance. Russia was beginning to follow suit, but the oak that will in years to come defy so many storms and shelter so many lives is as yet a sapling. We must face the bitter truth that had all our sisters accepted feminism we would have saved man from his worst enemy, we could have saved him from himself.

We could have said—

"We brought you into the world, we fed you at the breast, we guarded your tender years. When you grew older we gave you inspiration and the love that is the romance of life. We bore you children through agonies of which you know nothing; we loved you with the love that is woman's whole existence. You shall not destroy yourself, for you are ours and we are yours, and we are placed on this earth to lift it nearer to heaven, not to drag it down into hell. Your bits of shining metal or ribbons, your uniforms, your personal bravery are as nothing to us, if to earn the one or prove the other you are to kill and maim our husbands and sons, our fathers and brothers. There are greater fights to be fought, nobler victories to be won, and in the only war worth waging we can move by your side. Love and not hate must rule the world."

The time will come when woman will speak to man in this wise, and he will listen because he must, even though in listening he remove the strange, obscene gods of strife from his Pantheon. That the truth is known already to noble-minded women throughout the world is to me the most vitalising comfort that these days can yield. That so many women still pass it by, that they praise war and magnify personal courage and "martial glory," that they still foster and encourage the meanest

hatreds born of war, is I think worse than many a
disaster. But the lesson it enforces is plain. The
time is not ripe; before she can handle the power
to which she lays claim woman must abjure her
idols, she must follow the path of pain and suffering a little longer, she must learn for herself
through bitter experience how great a curse war is.
I believe she is learning her lesson; I believe that
the hosts of the unthinking are melting, and that as
the real meaning of glory, heroism and the rest is
brought home to her she will understand.

Even men in the lands of death and desolation
have been vouchsafed a glimpse of the truth. There
is nothing quite so pathetic in modern history as
that mingling of foes on Christmas Day, 1914, in
a brief truce of God. Truly the light was brief and
soon withdrawn, not to be rekindled a year later,
but it was strong enough to testify to the brotherhood of man obscured so long by kings and statesmen.

Women can rekindle the light so that it will not
be suddenly put out; they have no nobler purpose
under heaven. And in the days when they are
come to their full stature the memory of those
who applauded strife and were dazzled by some of
its exterior aspects will be utterly and happily forgotten.

XV

RACE SUICIDE

I was visiting the north of England in connection with an Industrial Congress, and I called upon a woman whose husband worked in a mine. Her small house was scrupulously clean, she was young, vigorous, swift in thought and movement, and gave me the impression that nothing came into her life in the form of obstacle and surprise without finding her ready to deal with it effectively. She showed me with a certain pride the small collection of books on social subjects bought in second-hand shops by her and her husband. I remember seeing John Stuart Mill, Ruskin, William Morris, Rowntree, Henry George, and many another familiar name. "We have read them together," she told me, "we have educated one another since the time we first met at evening classes." I remarked that her married life seemed to lack one thing only, and that was a family, and I quoted the Eastern aphorism that a house without children is a garden without flowers. She smiled a little sadly, and then I noted how some faint lines about her mouth tightened and hardened, robbing her of a certain charm. "Lady Warwick," she said, "we earn between us by hard work from day to day between four and five pounds a week. It has taken many years to reach that figure, and there is no chance of passing beyond it. What we have endured on the road to this comparative comfort we alone know, and we don't talk about it. But we both believe that the game is not worth the candle. The conditions of life in England are not worth perpetuating, and neither of us would willingly bring children into the world to take their chance and run their horrible risks as we did." She stopped for a moment in order to be sure of her self-control, and then she told me that in her view, though all her heart cried out for little children, sterility was the only protest that could be made against the cruel conditions of modern life under capitalism. "I know that my husband and I are desirables from the employer's standpoint. We earn far more than we receive, we are temperate, hardworking, punctual, reliable. But when we have settled our rent and rates, clubs, and insurances, dressed ourselves, paid tram fares and bought a few books, there is nothing left but a slender margin that a few months' illness would sweep away. For a week or ten days a year we may learn that England is not all as hideous as this corner of it, but we shall die without a glimpse of the world beyond and of its treasures that our books tell us about. If we stop to think, our life is full of unsatisfied longings, and though we don't give them free play we can't ignore them altogether. So we will not produce any more slaves for the capitalist, *and I can tell you that there is not one decently educated, young married woman of my acquaintance who is not of the same mind.* You could go into a score of houses known to me in this town alone and find strong, vigorous women whose childlessness is their one possible protest against the existing wage slavery."

Years have passed since, in that gloomy little northern town with its congeries of mean streets looking meaner than ever under the rain, I met the speaker whose name has passed from me. She may well be approaching the time when Nature will confirm her resolve irrevocably, but the memory of that conversation has haunted me with the vision of thousands of lost souls and unhappy lives.

I know now, if I did not know it then, that the music of little voices and the patter of little feet would have brought into that poor worker's life many of the joys for which she sighed in vain. She did not know, nor at that time did I, that obedience to natural law ensures a happiness that is independent of external circumstances, while disobedience brings in its train an ever-growing mental discord and sows the seeds of disease and decay. Statistics can be fascinating friends even though they be formidable acquaintances; they have a rough eloquence of their own that is more effective than honeyed speech.

The birth-rate of England, France, and the United States, associated as it is in all these countries with the death-rate of the newly born, is to me one of the most depressing signs of the times. I cannot help realising that in many cases sterility is not the deliberate protest of the wage slave, it is the selfish protest of the pleasure seeker, and in a small minority of cases the genuine, yet narrow, fear of the eugenist and his following whose enthusiasms have outrun both knowledge and faith. Tolstoy went so far as to say that the man who enjoys association with his wife for any purpose save procreation is guilty of a crime. While many childless women live celibate lives, particularly in America, the great majority do not. In Milton's stately words they "of love and love's delight take freely," as though the power that rules and guides the world could in the long run be outwitted by what it has created.

To-day the civilised world is at the parting of the ways. War has riven asunder the ranks of the

best and bravest, and has left in the hearts of the
survivors so vivid a sense of the horrors of life
that many a man will hesitate to become a father
lest his sons have to take their place in time to
come on the fields of war and his daughters chance
to be among the dwellers in a conquered city. All
classes have been gathered to battle, one and all
will feel the responsibility attending the failure of
our civilisation. While many will believe they are
responding to a high instinct when they elect to follow the line of least resistance and leave the world
a little poorer, the cumulative effect of such a decision is positively terrible to contemplate.

There are some lines in *Coriolanus* that might
have been addressed not to those who banished him
from Rome, but to the women of the world's most
highly civilised countries:—

> "Have the power still
> To banish your defenders; till at length
> Your ignorance, which finds not till it feels,
> Making not reservation of yourselves,
> Still your own foes, deliver you as most
> Abated captives to some nation
> That won you without blows."

If these lines are really as appropriate as they
seem to me, it is because the women of the civilised world and the more leisured section of it are
on their trial. There is going to be an unimagined

shortage among the best elements of the most highly civilised population, a shortage due in part to the fashion in which responsible women have neglected their duties hitherto. If the pleasure lovers decline their share of child-bearing on the ground that it robs them of long periods of amusement, and if the finest type of women workers refuse on the other grounds raised earlier in this paper, what will be the result? There will be a sharp social cleavage, the few clever exploiters will enchain the unfit who are produced so rapidly, we shall develop a small class that governs and a large class that is ruled, all progress will come to an end, while the conditions obtaining when the industrial era was opened by steam power will be revived with all the attendant horrors in some new and unsuspected guise.

It is well to remember how, following the first trumpet call of war, our hard-won liberties were stripped from us. Some of my American friends say it is because our free institutions were not very deeply rooted, but I am well convinced that if the United States were involved, the results would be much the same. War always dethrones Liberty, and the nation that can set her up again when peace is restored may be congratulated. As a rule the struggle has to begin all over again, for the State advances claims that are incompatible with any kind of freedom that is worth having. Only the will of the people can gain liberty, and to make that will sufficiently strong and effective it must be expressed by the best human material, the children of the best types. So it seems to me that race suicide, evil at all times, becomes in seasons like this an act of treason, not only to the nation but to civilisation and all those ideals upon which civilisation waits.

In the town to which I referred on the first page of this paper, the women who deliberately discarded motherhood might between them have raised a strong company to fight for the rights of the next generation. They were shocked to consider the travail that brought them beyond the reach of want, had they lost sympathy with those who succumbed by the way? Is not the fate of these last the more tragic?

The faults and failures of life are not a divine dispensation. Providence has placed us in a marvellous world, capable of raising far more than is needed to supply the reasonable wants of one and all. That there are misery, injustice, want and inequality must not be charged to the account of Providence, but to the foolishness and immortal greed of man, who cannot deal equitably with the resources of which he is the trustee. The world waxes richer year by year, for we are gathering the power to increase production and to distribute

the surplus of one region to supply the deficiency
of another. It is a very fair and beautiful world,
and we need no more than that all should be permitted to share what is produced. To enforce this
distribution, to see that it is enjoyed in peace and
tranquillity is the appointed task of a strong and
vigorous democracy. The primal duty of women is
to give this democracy to the world and keep its
strength renewed.

Some may fear that women "condemned to fer-
tility" as one phrased it in my hearing recently, may
be unable to take their part in the struggle for
emancipation. But surely motherhood enforces the
qualifications of women, justifies their claims and
provides them with the material to train for future
triumphs. Olive Schreiner, in her magnificent book
"Woman and Labour," in which, however, she
wrote of the birth-rate and its incidents without
visualising the possibilities of world war, says that
some birds have raised the union of the sexes to a
far higher level than humanity has reached. The
male and the female share the nest building, the
incubation and the feeding of the young, and it
was impossible for that fine observer to note any
difference in the task of the sexes. So it should
be with us and will be when we have developed to
that standard. The labours and responsibilities of
the home, and the daily work will be a part of the

common contract and bond of men and women, and
no woman will be disqualified by the fulfilment of
her duties in the home more than the man is disqualified by reason of his labours beyond it. We
are all conscious of evils that throng the world,
we all strive to better them in a degree, few of
the most careless fail altogether to be kind in some
fashion, however haphazard, but if the women who
take life seriously will not only fulfil the command-
ment to be fruitful and multiply, but will do their
best to urge their reluctant sisters, a single generation may avail to restore the balance of sanity,
equity and progress throughout civilisation.

This social disease of race suicide has not been
long established. It came into France, I believe,
as a result of the law that divides the inheritance
of the parents among the children equally, it has
crept into England and America chiefly as a
product of overmuch luxury and wealth. Apart
from such a reason as calculated protest against
social inequalities, it is due to the methods of life
that soften women and make child-bearing a terror. I have been told by my travelled friends, the
men and women who have been to the far ends of
the earth, that in the lands where women are hardy,
healthy, and vigorous, there is no trouble for the
mother at these critical times. She recovers her full
strength in a few days. At Easton, in Essex, where

I was born and brought up, and at Warwick, where I have lived so much since my marriage, I have seen that the workers' wives who live frugally and actively are able to rear large families and retain not only their health, but their good looks. Casting my memory back I can recall the time when great families were the rule, and not the exception, among the leisured classes. The women who entertained in great houses that they administered in every detail, brought their six, eight, or ten children into the world and lived long, healthy, happy lives. The modern fashion is of recent date, and now that the war has stirred the heights and depths of human consciousness the old bad custom should pass, for the sake of a world that the madmen of mankind have made desolate. At no period in the history of Western civilisation, has it been more necessary for the women who count as factors in world progress to consider their duty and fulfil it to the extreme limit of their power.

I think that the need of the United States is not less than our own, for it sees the influx day by day of the most diverse elements, and knows well enough that the genius of rule belongs to the Anglo-Saxon. The negroid element does not forget its duty, and the honest class of immigrant that seeks to share the benefit of an enlightened civilisation is hardly less prolific. Against all the problems that my American friends, and they are many, have set out, there is no surer safeguard than an ever increasing birth-rate of the best elements.

I have never felt disposed to join in the cry of the Yellow Peril, nor to think well of those who raise it wantonly, but certain facts stand out in a very bright light shed upon them by the war. In the first place the Allied powers of the Entente have sought the services of both yellow and black races, and have by so doing proclaimed the dawn of a new era in which all questions of equality must come to the front. Japan is very wide awake, and China is still a slumbering giant. Given sanitary science and a great gift of organisation, she might rule all Asia. The Berbers, Arabs, and negroid races of Africa have lined our trenches and taken part in our attacks; one and all, to say nothing of the Indian soldiers, have learned more of war in the past year or so than they had ever known before. They have seen the weakness as well as the strength of the white man.

Black and yellow races alike are extraordinarily prolific; there is among their women no shirking of duty in that regard. Very soon the white man will realise that he cannot maintain his old position unless he is fully prepared to accept responsibilities far greater than those of his forebears. If the rate of his progression falls while that of the other races rises, there can only be one solution in the end, such a solution as "Coriolanus" speaks of in the scathing lines I have quoted. In short, if the white man's burden is to be borne there must be sufficient white men to bear it. Statesmen will labour in vain and the friends of progress will strive to no end if the start that the other races have gained is to be increased, and the white women of the world must decide whether or no they are content that not only their own nation but the whole standard of life for which they stand is to be submerged, or whether by a generous interpretation of the duties of motherhood they will enable their people to remain in the future as they have been in the past. We cannot tell what the final harvest of war will amount to, but with the dead, the diseased and the disabled, it will probably run into ten figures, more than five times the measure of human sacrifice demanded by all the great wars that shook the world from Blenheim to Omdurman. Even these monstrous figures do not tell the whole tale, for there will be among the dead, thousands of men whose talent might have developed into genius, and there will be hundreds of thousands of widows left in the full flush of womanhood, with all their possibilities unfulfilled, and, in countless cases, beyond the reach of fulfilment. To put it brutally, our civilisation that stands in bitter need of its best breeding stock has deliberately slaughtered a very large percentage of it.

This, indeed, is race suicide in its worst form, and just as woman hopes by her emancipation to dam the tide of war, so she must step into the breach and dam the tide of loss. Emancipation will do very little for women if when they have obtained it they find the best elements of the white races increasingly unable to stand the strain imposed by war. They will not forget that the black man's women are bought to tend his land and enable him to live in ease or that the Mohammedan in the enforced seclusion of the harem may share his favours among four lawful wives and as many concubines as his purse can furnish. As the standard of civilisation declines, woman, by reason of her physical weakness, must pay an ever increasing penalty; only when it has risen to heights unreached before the war may she hope to come into her own and to realise ambitions that, dormant or active, have been with her through the centuries. The whole question of her future has been brought by the war outside the domain of personal or even national interests, suddenly it has become racial.

Down to a little while ago the solution was not in woman's hands, to-day it belongs to her, she has to decide not only for herself, but for all white mankind. It is not too much to say that civilisation, as we know it, will soon be waiting upon her verdict. If this statement seems too far reaching, if it seems to challenge probability, let those who think so turn to any good history of the world and see for themselves how each civilisation has been overwhelmed as soon as it reached the limits of its efficiency and endurance. In the history of this planet, changes no less sweeping than that which I have indicated have been recorded, the Providence that has one race or colour in its special keeping is but the offspring of our own conceit. The real Providence that dominates the universe treats all the races on their merits. If, and only if, the best types of women will embrace motherhood ardently, bravely content to endure the discomforts and discover for themselves the infinite pleasure, can the earth, as we know it, survive the terrible shock it has received. Even then the recovery will be slow, and the price to be paid will be bitter beyond imagining, but we shall in the end win through, though I who write and you who read may well have settled our account with mortality before the season of full recovery dawns upon a wasted world. Should we fail in our duty then we must pass as Babylon and Egypt and Rome passed before us, to become no more than mere shadows of a name.

The least among us may dream dreams and see visions. My own dream and my own vision are of woman as the saviour of the race. I see her fruitful womb replenish the wasted ranks, I hear her wise counsels making irresistibly attractive the flower-strewn ways of peace. I see the few women who encourage war turning from the error of their ways, and those who have spurned motherhood realising before it is too late the glory of their neglected burden. And I believe with a faith that nothing can shake that with these two changes and a wise recognition that the fruits of the earth were given to us all not in accordance with our gifts, but in the measure of our needs, a new season may come to this distracted world. Should all the high hopes of our noblest suffer eclipse, should all the travail of the Christian era be brought to nothingness? I have too much faith in my sex to believe it will let the world perish if the real meaning and significance of its duty can be brought home to it. We have been ill educated, we have been spoilt, we have been corrupted, but for all that there is a certain soundness at the heart of woman. She has not shrunk from the duties she understands, even the lapse from grace that recent years have revealed will not outlive this understanding.

The responsibility for spreading the truth rests upon all who recognise it. There are countless women throughout the world who by sheer force of character can influence their women friends and have learned that the vital problem of sex is not rightly to be treated as though it were not fit for discussion. They are scattered over all the cities of the world; the cumulative effect of their labours would be immense, irresistible. I am sure that the perils I have outlined are known and feared in the Old World and the New, that they are mentioned in the highest quarters of London, Paris, and Washington, and that the transitional period separating words from deeds must needs be brief because the problem does not brook delay. Many women will respond without questioning to the call of duty. Some, whose life struggle can be understood only by those who share it, may ask first that their offspring shall be treated as what they are, State assets, and not abandoned to all the evils of poverty. Others will want to know that they are not raising sons to become the "cannon fodder" of kings and statesmen. In the light of the needs of the white man's world, and the weight of the white man's burden, are even these assurances too much to ask?

XVI

IT came upon me with a sudden sense of revelation, for when I went into the theatre my thoughts were heavy with the weight of war. The friend with whom I had dined had insisted, and though at first I had refused, she had compromised with my objections. "Come and see some pictures, if you cannot face a three-act play," she had said. "I can promise you something quite remarkable, and when you have had enough, just rise and I will follow." But in the end it was my friend who suggested leaving, because she had a long day's work before her and knew that I too had an engagement nearly two hundred miles from town. And when I told her that she had shown me more than she herself had seen, and that I would not have missed that couple of hours' illumination on any account, she merely said she would not attempt to understand, but was very glad.

I have been greatly concerned with problems of peace and war from the woman's view-point. So many women have written to me about the question, some from far-away corners of the States, others from remote English country-sides. I feel the ferment in the blood of every thinking woman; I know how surely and inevitably the time is coming when men and women must face the problem of world control side by side. It has seemed to me that only one force can avail to end war, and that is the force of education supplementing the efforts and strengthening the bands of brotherhood. But how should one make the dry bones of education live for those to whom education is now no more than dry bones? We can reach the children whose imagination is yet immature, how reach the grown up, immersed in the struggle for life and bringing even to their leisure the harassed mind and tired brain? How make the path clear, how stir to the depths their slumbering sense of the world that lies beyond their working day? When I went into the Scala Theatre in London the problem was a baffling one, when I had seen "The Birth of a Nation" I realised the truth that such pictures in the hands of men with insight and vision may yet move the world.

We of England may well forget the follies of our forebears, and the American with Anglo-Saxon blood in his veins may well forgive them, while both tingle with pride at the accomplishment of those "Mayflower" Pilgrims who paved the way for the

coming of a nation destined I think in the near
future to become the wealthiest, most powerful, and,
one hopes, the most progressive on the face of the
earth. But who realised, save in a vague and uncertain fashion, the true glory of America's brief history? Who could visualise the scenes to which
statesmen and orators recur from time to time? Of
the general public few indeed if any, to the rank
and file the experience of seeing the past flower into
life before them must have been such a one as Keats
describes—

> "Then felt I like some watcher of the skies
> When a new planet swims into his ken,
> Or like stout Cortez when with eagle eyes
> He star'd at the Pacific—and all his men
> Look'd at each other with a wild surmise
> Silent, upon a peak in Darien."

A few deep thinkers, men with vivid minds, must
of course have seen beyond the limited vision of
the multitude, or nothing so sweepingly compre-
hensive, so splendidly realistic, so artistically complete as "The Birth of a Nation" could have been
devised. It is poetry almost in the sense that
Hardy's "Dynasts" is poetry, while its educational
value, appealing as it can to young and old, learned
and illiterate alike, is very real. Whatever the commercial value, and this I am glad to think must be
great, the value of the spectacle as a force for the

promotion of the highest order of patriotism is greater still. I can only feel delighted to think that such a task could be so carefully undertaken and so satisfactorily achieved.

A picture play may not seem at first sight a very great medium for presenting the truth about history or even a single facet of the great diamond of life; at least if I am honest with myself this would have been my own opinion down to the date of my visit to "The Birth of a Nation." I had misjudged the scope of the picture play in the light of the hoardings, vulgar, fantastic, or silly, that make the streets of even the small provincial towns more than necessarily offensive. I did not understand that in the hands of capable and imaginative artists, not only the present can be put before us, but the past can be reconstructed, and the future suggested. How it would help us to understand not only ourselves, but others of the great group of nations if we could see the history of all countries presented with something of the skill and sincerity that have gone to these graphic outlines of America's past! Often in Warwick Castle, as I have pondered some of the records of bygone time and half-forgotten history, I have marvelled at the pageant that is suggested, but never realised by the pages before me. If we could bring our history before ourselves would it not teach us more of our triumphs and mistakes

than any book? And if the history of the struggles
and endeavours of other nations could be faithfully
presented, would there not be in the vision something to make us more sympathetic, more ready to
realise that we are all passing along the same road,
a narrow bridge of consciousness spanning the river
of life that flows through eternity, with dreamless
sleep or life beyond our ken on either hand? Would
it not help to teach us that for the people of every
race that brief spell of consciousness is associated
with so many self-made troubles that the hell of
the obsolete theologians is rendered quite superfluous? We cannot in normal times hate the men,
women, and children of another race merely because
they are not of our own. The same virtues, the
same strivings, the same uprising towards the elu-
sive light are shared in common. So, too, are the
prejudices and errors with which we strive. Presented with sympathy, and, above all, with humility,
the history of the birth and subsequent struggle of
all the nations would be a potent force for peace,
because it would be the first aid to understanding.

I think that the men and women who have paid
their vows to peace, those who, while realising that
the present war must go on to the end, will make
any sacrifice to deprive it of a successor, may find in
the picture play, carefully conditioned to the needs
of our fateful times, the fulcrum that will enable

them to move the world. I can see it passing from the domain of the theatre to the lecture hall. I can see the best features of the enterprise enlarged and developed until at last the benefits of travel and a knowledge of history are put before those who under normal conditions—or rather the conditions that the Moloch of commercialism has made normal —would never be able to enjoy either. I hold and shall always hold, that the ultimate power of directing their lives is in the hands of the people, it is not rightly in the gift of Kings or Kaisers, diplomats, statesmen, or soldiers. The sunrise of peace waits upon the dawn of knowledge, of knowledge that can be acquired by men, women and grown-up children of the working classes, the classes that accomplish all that is worth accomplishing, and pay the fullest penalty of the greed and vanity of those who live upon their labours. But, as I have so often insisted, the workers are inarticulate, particularly in the southern counties and round the metropolis of England; they do not breathe the fresh air of the north, and it is notorious that London ruins the breed of the workers. The greater the city, the greater the unemployment, the keener the competition, the readier the acceptance of conditions that make men the slaves instead of the masters of their task, the smaller the leisure to think or to study the curious and manifold complexities of ex-

isting conditions. Only by making that study easy
and by giving it the form of relaxation, by stimulating the tired brain, can the worker be roused.
It is a matter of fact rather than of conjecture, that
the picture "palace" is beginning to claim his scanty
leisure, and his tiny surplus over the paramount demands of a minimum of food and clothing. Democratic in its essence and secure in its appeal, it seems
to me that the picture theatre can be developed to
the most instructive and useful ends. It can teach
the working man the history of his own career and
long struggle towards fairer conditions of life and
labour, it can show the world's workers all aiming
to reach the same legitimate goal and it can enforce
the lesson that a unity of ideals, and a stern rejection of the counsels of those who would make
mankind his enemies rather than his friends will
make war impossible. It may be that in America,
that great melting-pot, as Mr. Zangwill calls it,
of all jarring nationalities, the lesson is more obvious and more quickly mastered, but there is a
work well-nigh as great to be done in England,
where if the mixing of the nationalities is less noticeable, the need for knowledge is still greater.
The States, wealthy beyond the dreams of avarice,
entirely self-supporting, and utterly unchallenged
by any Power within striking distance, may well

laugh in the face of those who would impose upon them the extravagant horrors of militarism.

We shall have to face militarism over here; it has had its advocates for many years, and—why deny it?—their position will be immensely strengthened by the war. We know by now that our rulers cannot save us, that if we would be saved it must be by ourselves, and we know too that salvation will be born of knowledge and of knowledge alone. I regard the picture theatre as the finest medium for the spread of knowledge now before the public, and I am confident that if the great engineers of enterprise will devote their energies to the sane peace propaganda that consists in showing not only the history but the aims of the great majority of civilised people, the lesson will travel far and sink deep. "The Birth of a Nation" reveals the infinite capacity of the master film makers, their resource and resources, the measure of skill they can command. It also shows by reason of its success the immense public interest, the desire to learn, and to make use of knowledge. It is not often that a venture avowedly commercial in its aims can perform a world-wide service, and I am optimistic enough to believe that those in charge of such a work as that which is responsible for my own conversion and enthusiasm will be quick to see that in serving themselves they can serve humanity.

XVII

It seems only a few years since Truth, if not precisely popular, enjoyed a certain reputation, a little definite vogue. To tell the truth, the whole truth and nothing but the truth was not only a nominal obligation in the courts of law, but a tradition among a certain class, small but not negligible, of English men and women. Truth was found in all sorts of places, you met it sometimes in Parliament, generally on the back benches, now and again it was seen or suspected in the Press; it frequented the Pulpit, and was not unknown upon the public platform if the gathering was not one of the political rallies that it resolutely ignored. To be sure when intended for the appreciation or admiration of sensitive folk, it was always dressed up in garments that hid a part of its native ugliness, and over the hard, unrelenting features a certain veil, enforcing a decent obscurity, was scrupulously drawn. The higher Truth climbed in the social scale, the more the trappings, the thicker the veil, while on the lowest rungs of the social ladder there

were none to supply dress or wrappings, and Truth
stood revealed in such an ugly guise that only
the strong minded dared to look. When they told
what they had seen, all those who lived on any of
the rungs above them deplored at the top of their
voices the indecency of the revelation and devised
thicker veils and heavier drapery. And yet for all
men and all women, according to their capacity for
looking courageously before them, Truth existed.
Among most of those who live in comfort there was
a tradition that Truth had borrowed the head of
Medusa the Gorgon lady who incontinently turned
to stone all those who looked upon her, and was
ultimately tricked out of life and activity by Per-
seus; on the other hand, the people of the under-
world, the world that does the rough work, had
looked upon Truth and found the cold implacable
eyes had in them more of stimulus than death.
They even went so far as to hope that in times yet
to come the robing and veiling of Truth would be
regarded as an offence and the duty of looking
Truth straight in the face, would be obligatory
upon kings, statesmen, clergymen, county· and
district councillors, journalists and lawyers alike.
Against the gross indelicacy of this democratic suggestion there was not unnaturally a revolt, as many
of those people just mentioned had every reason
to fear that such a decision would rob them of oc-

cupations that, if not actually profitable to their
fellow-men, were at least sometimes dignified and
very often lucrative.

Then came War, and the people of all combatant
countries formed amid and despite their bitter antagonisms an unwritten, unsigned compact to the
effect that whatever the divergence of their aims
and policies, they would at least conduct one part
of their campaign in common, against a common
foe. Agreements having lost their validity, it was
impossible to reduce this one to writing, and they
knew, too, that actions speak louder than words.
So with unanimity that forgot all causes of dis-
pute, the fighting powers found time and means
and occasion in the midst of their awful traffic to
wage war against Truth. In this country the naked
Truth may no longer find a resting place, if the
well in which Truth is said to dwell could be located it would incontinently be filled up and no
material would be regarded as too poisonous for
the purpose. As the well cannot be located, the
Defence of the Realm Act has, in these islands in-
stituted sumptuary laws so strict that Truth is now
robed, veiled, and manacled past recognition. The
delight of those who have suffered from the constant fear of the apparition, who have found their
enjoyment of the feast of life constantly menaced
by the report that Truth was in the neighbourhood,

is unbounded. It is admitted by every government that Truth is one of the greatest obstacles to the proper progress of universal destruction and all Governments have substituted in the interests of public digestion Fiction, a far more popular creation and more palatable too. They call it by the title of Official Report. If one Report contradicts and is contradicted by all the others, you can at least pay your money and take your choice and the task of selection is eased by the certain knowledge that Truth is not admitted to any.

In the Parliaments of the world responsible speakers have but to declare that the irresponsible ones are endeavouring to bring back Truth to the high assembly, and every one of Fiction's countless adherents will rise in his place to protest. In the pulpit, to which Truth still seeks admittance, the veil has become a mask, and the garments have a double thickness, but in the Courts of whatever kind and in Fleet Street it has been found that the precautions in vogue before the war are sufficiently adequate.

To any mortal such persecution had been fatal, but Truth is immortal and persists. Not even the Jews whose sufferings are eternal, or the Belgians, Poles, Armenians, Servians, and others whose persecution though intolerable is temporary, strive to recover their vanished freedom as resolutely as

Truth. The harder you use it, the greater its persistence. Drive it out at the door it returns by the window, an indefatigable, untiring immortal, seemingly unconscious of the loss of popularity, convinced that it has a place in the great scheme of things. It whispers to kings on their thrones, and to chancellors in their studies, to statesmen on Government and opposition benches, to clergymen in their pulpits, lawyers in their consulting rooms; passing by janitor, secretary, and a sub-editorial array, it even invades the editor's desk, persistent though ignored. Trampled upon, cast aside, ignored, eviscerated, turned inside out, confuted, obscured, denied, perverted, misunderstood and damned, it still labours, powerful as in the days when old Thomas Carlyle watched its progress through the world and hailed it alone immortal. With a striking disregard of the laws of emergency and confusion, it declines to be regarded as an enemy alien. With an utter contempt for a Fiction entrenched behind all the barbed wires of popularity, it whispers the most disconcerting statements to those who hoped or believed that it was dead. None can say what form the instructions, warnings, and admonitions take, but all may guess them, and the temptation so to do is ever present.

I think that the one outstanding fact upon which

Truth insists is that until it is allowed to prevail there can be no peace in the world, that even victories must be unavailing while the hard-won lessons they bring are taught in terms of fiction. Truth tells us that the fog of war is hardly more horrible than the fog of falsehood; product of a poison gas that is manufactured by every country alike. To the Prussians who are in our midst striving to fasten upon us the fetters fashioned by our enemies for the control of all liberty, comes the secret warning that such fetters will not fit the Anglo-Saxon people, that the rivets will not hold, that they will be torn asunder and even used as weapons against all forgers. Truth will tell those who seek to effect economies at the expense of education that only sound training and diligent application to every form of activity can enable us to hold our own against Germany, whether the defeat of that country be whole or partial. Truth says the will of the people is being forged as of wrought iron upon the fields of war, and that the days of privilege are numbered. Truth whispers that the burdens imposed upon those yet unborn, not only in Great Britain, but in every belligerent country can only be met if they are shared by one and all, not with any sense of precedence or class distinction but in a brotherhood that embraces all who labour whether with hand or brain to the common end.

Truth will whisper to those who shrink before strong, whole-hearted and courageous methods necessary to bring all classes into line that the needs of the time are paramount and that those who will not steer the ship of State to a safe harbour because of the adverse winds and storming waves that lie ahead, must yield to other pilots cast in sterner mould. It will point out that the old days of political trifling and dalliance are numbered, that right and wrong, bravery and cowardice, energy and inaction, whatever their future, can no longer be weighed in the unjust balances of the party system. Truth will say that our empire needs the best service, not only of every man, but of every woman, and in consequence, that both must be rendered fit to serve and allowed to express themselves to the State's best advantage without reference to pedigree or sex. It will declare that an England in which the labours of six men out of seven are valued at three pounds a week or under, cannot endure for the simple reason that under the present social system, hundreds of thousands of really capable people who could deserve well of their country are doomed by poverty to ineffectiveness. Truth will say bluntly that the future demands statesmen rather than politicians, men in their prime rather than men in their decline. It will whisper of the vigorous democracies that the genius

of empire has brought into being, the democracies
that have striven so nobly to save the empire and
must—not for reasons of sentiment alone—play
their part in administering it. There will not be
wanting the reminder that the season in which
crises, military, social, political, can be smothered
in platitudes is past, not in our time to return.

If Truth were to proclaim these facts duly
pointed and applied, together with many another
of like weight and significance from the house-tops,
the Defence of the Realm Act would intervene
promptly, strongly and passionately on behalf of
Fiction; but the Act has limitations. The Still
Small Voice evades the Act every time, it speaks
less from the lips than to the hearts of men. There
is no humbug so highly placed as to be able to
shut it out, there is no man or woman so befogged
or bewildered by the horror of the hour that he cannot hear the silences made audible. For Truth is
not cast out of life, it is but despised and rejected
by the world's rulers and even they cannot shut
out the voice that whispers through all their waking
hours, for while many men can deceive others, few,
if any, are permitted entirely to deceive themselves
in times like these. So many soft conventions have
fallen by the way, so many of life's excuses and
subterfuges have fallen into everlasting nothingness. Before the horror-stricken eyes of authority

the world over, Truth, muzzled, bedraped, masked, and shrouded appears again like the skeleton at the feast, like the grinning skull that accompanied the Roman Emperors on their Triumphs to remind them that they too were mortal. Slowly yet with deliberation Truth is beginning to shed the coverings that officialdom had heaped in such designed profusion. The day is not far distant when the fetters will fall from the limbs, the shroud from the dread face, and in that hour not all the Acts and Proscriptions will avail to frame a covering. Europe, bleeding, sore, wounded, poverty-stricken, shattered beyond recognition, will see Truth face to face. And then——?

XVIII

I HAVE been trying to look through the clouds of war to what lies behind. Quite resolutely I have closed my ears to certain empty cries about the commercial conquest of Germany, about the coming of Protection, about all the panaceas of political and other quacks. Most of us who take the trouble to think can trace these cries to their source. I have endeavoured to look to the time when this old country of ours will be faced by a new set of conditions, by forces yet incalculable that war has brought into being. People have talked and written glibly about changes of heart, of the fraternising of capital and labour, of sin and crime and disease exorcised by some supreme spirit of good will, but I have my doubts. "Cœlum non animum mutant," wrote Horace, two thousand years ago.

Men have always made good resolutions in times of stress; they range from the nation's ideals voiced by its spokesmen down to the promise of candles for the shrine of some saint. The mind can follow the road that connects our English House of Com-

mons or the Russian home of the Duma with the
church of Notre Dame de la Garde whereto the
men who traffic in the mighty waters of the Gulf
of Lyons pay with knick-knacks for their real or
imaginary protection. I have no faith in the power
of good intentions to act automatically. When
this war is over and we are faced with a victory,
an indecisive result, or a defeat, the tendency of
our insularity will be to interfere as little as may
be with pre-existing conditions. Men who serve
in high places will be overwrought; you do not carry
a part of the burden of the British Empire upon
your shoulders without a maximum of strain. The
tendency will, I fear, be to declare that the evil
of the day is sufficient, that the nation must be kept
secure from new ideas. There will be few to make
excursion in search of trouble. Yet there can be
very few students of social progress who will not
admit that the only way in which we can make
good the losses of war, is by turning to the best possible account the assets left to us at its conclusion.
And the supreme asset of a State is its children.

Let us leave aside for the moment all the other
burning social questions of the time. They are not
the less poignant because a great patriotic impulse
has kept so much suffering silent. The question
of the future of our great Empire is one that must
be decided in a large measure by those who are chil-

dren to-day. We have to ask ourselves what we are doing to prepare them for their labours, and how far such preparation can bear comparison with that made by the nations which will be our competitors. We are the trustees of the British Empire, Unlimited. What manner of estate are we going to bequeath to our children?

Down to the summer of 1914, we had every means of doing well for the generation that must grasp the reins when at Time's bidding we relinquish them. That we had misused those means goes without saying. As far as education goes it was said years ago of our richest schools that a vast sum of money was expended on education, and that a beggarly account of empty brains was the result. That indictment holds good to-day. The education of the children of the wealthy is both costly and ineffective. Much that is taught bears no relation to the needs of twentieth-century life. Middle class education is better without being good, while the State education that, as far as the poor is concerned, is both obligatory and free, is worth what it costs. Secondary Education is pursued if at all under conditions of the greatest difficulty. Boys and girls too under our present evil economic conditions are turned into wage-earners at the earliest possible moment. County Council classes, often capably conducted and well within the reach of the great majority, cannot find adequate support for many reasons. One is that the primary education of the poor does not encourage the habit of study. The ill-fed children of the slums look upon school as a necessary evil, redeemed to a small extent by the gift of free meals, over which, we, the richest nation of the earth, haggled so long. When the children of the poor have reached the standard or the age that sets them free, the struggle for life begins and finds them too jaded at the end of the normal day's work to seek fresh instruction, even if they have an inclination or ambition to improve their minds. Untrained, undisciplined, condemned in many instances to blind-alley employment, what better is to be expected? Again we are face to face with the demand for cheap labour, the labour that enriches the employer and even gives an illusory benefit to the State. Save in the direction of making laws, most of them foolish, and raising money, much of it ill spent, the State follows a policy of *laissez faire*. The effort to make primary education compulsory has seemingly left it without the energy to see that it should also be sound and effective. The latter-day squabbles between Church and State in the schoolroom have always been regarded as more interesting than education itself. Legislators by the score have shown in Parliament that the question of feeding hungry children so that they may be physically fit to learn, is the only side of education over which they are prepared to spend any thought, and that in order to oppose action. So these things were down to the time when England went to war, so they will be after England returns to peace unless the great body of public opinion in the country will realise that no victory can be enduring if countries anxious to compete with us in the future give a genuine education to their children while we remain content with a spurious one for ours. The issue cannot be evaded; the responsibility cannot be shirked. French education, German, Dutch, Danish, and Swiss are better than ours. They take into account the needs of the times. They are not founded upon old and obsolete prejudices. The technical side of educational needs is fairly and fully met. The State equipment is better. The teachers know that there are people in the world who do not speak English, and that several European languages not only have a claim to consideration, but must be taught by competent masters; that is to say, by men and women with a liberal education born in the land whose language they teach. Travelling scholarships should be the first reward of those who excel at school. The incentive would be immense, and the contribution to the forces of peace immeasurable.

Even our cousins across the Atlantic, who have made their educational system a living thing, have failed to teach us. Andrew Carnegie, remembering the land of his birth, has liberally endowed Scottish University Education with the gold of Pittsburg. Harvard, Yale, Princeton, and other American colleges are an example to the world, in Canada the lesson has been learned, in Toronto, Montreal and elsewhere, and will soon be fully applied. But here in England those who cannot go to Oxford or Cambridge will find that, for the most part, they must be external students in pursuit of the higher education, with little of the joyous intercourse that kindles ambitions and ideals. We look a little askance at education. For the man in the street the really great representatives of Cam and Isis are those who can row from Putney to Mortlake in the early spring, and those who can shine at the cricket ground in Marylebone about midsummer. Scholarship is something in the nature of a harmless eccentricity, calling less for rebuke than for derision. For this view-point our hopeless system of primary education is responsible. To be effective in this country education must be revised to meet the times we live in, made popular and finally democratised. As I write we are waging war at the price of some four or five million pounds a day. We must wage peace with as fine a disregard for inevitable expenditure. The cost of one week's war will maintain an entirely different system of national education for a year. I would like to deal in brief broad outline with what might be attempted.

It is only necessary to concede in the first instance that a sane Government recognises the paramount claims of the children, the terrible loss of much of the country's best blood, and the consequent need of bringing what is left to us to the highest pitch of public utility. These premises should surely stand beyond controversy. Why should not every slum child have its share of public-school life free of all charge? If we have come to the conclusion that this is the best thing for the future of the country, why should the majority of the little ones be left out? Does anybody hold that we do not require the best that all the children can do for England? To those who suggest that such a simple matter is revolutionary, or that it will cost too much, one reply is that our children are our greatest national asset. Upon our capacity to rear them well and wisely and to educate them to the needs of the time, the whole future of the British Empire depends. There is really nothing revolutionary about the proposal, for, if you come to think of it, we give free education and even free meals, and the most hardened Conservative will acknowledge freely enough that the slum is not a good training ground for the rising generation. You cannot clear slums away in a hurry. The owners of such places are regarded if not with affection, at least with respect by the law and the law makers, but you can run up boarding establishments that will be infinitely superior to slums, and you can gather within them the outcasts of the capitalistic system for proper feeding, clothing, education, and training. If children go wrong they are sent to special schools. All that is necessary is that instead of the children going wrong, the grown-ups shall go right, that they shall recognise how little their politics, prejudices and preconceptions matter by the side of one child's welfare. I go as far as to declare that it is the bounden duty of the State to make its gift of education effective, that in making education compulsory it recognised certain paramount duties that remain fulfilled only in the letter, and not in the spirit. One does not advocate change, however beneficial, for the mere sake of a nobler and wider life, such pleas do not gain prompt acceptance. Rather let it be stated quite frankly that, unless we turn the best aptitudes and capacities of the rising generation to the fullest account, we cannot hope to maintain our position in the face of competition. As a nation we handicap ourselves lamentably when we endeavour to hold our own in the world with no more than a small part of our national assets realised or realisable. Children are our assets, and between the infant mortality on the one hand, blind product of ignorance, poverty, and apathy, and indifferent education on the other hand, we stand a very bad chance in the battle for supremacy. If we would increase, preserve, and train child life we could look to the future without misgiving.

Edmund Burke, who will not be found to have given many hostages to socialism, declared that the citizens of a State are a partnership, that every member of such partnership has a right to a fair portion of all that society with all its combinations of skill and force can do in his favour, and that he has a right to the fruits of his own industry and the improvement of his own offspring. Let us be content to leave the case as Burke stated it in the time of George III., it will be seen that we have not yet gained for the average man the minima that the most eloquent statesman of his time prescribed. It is also clear that this claim for a full and free education is not the claim for charity, but the claim for a right that should be deemed inalienable. The grant of this right enriches while appearing to impoverish the State, and a step that some will deem socialistic and others revolutionary is fairly defined as common-sense procedure. We have at last reached the stage of agreeing that child life must be increased, preserved, and cultivated to the best ends, but there is a fatal inclination in this country to regard the theoretical acceptance of a principle as the equivalent of its complete practical development. When you discuss the whole vital question with sensible people they prove, almost without exception, in accord, but as soon as you say, *"therefore let us endow maternity, pass Pure Milk Bills, protect the mother from wrongful labour before and after confinement, and the child from mal-nutrition, educate the child when it is old enough to be educated, submit it to reasonable discipline and prepare it physically, morally, and mentally to fill the place for which it is best fitted in the workshop of the world,"* the theorists are unable to follow. Some constitutional timidity holds them. They will not gallop across country to reach their goal, fences and ditches frighten them, and all gates must be unfastened. It is well for those of us whose ambitions for England are inexhaustible, and who watch the shadow on Life's Dial moving inexorably towards the sunset that we dare not despair of humanity. The pen, however ill we may wield it, gives us courage. We know that when our views are issued broadcast they resemble the seed in the Parable of the Sower, and that some worker who in days yet unborn will lead the children of the poor to their safe harbour out of the troubled waters on which their helpless lives are tossed, will have gathered a part of his inspiration and force from the thoughts of those who have gone before.

What is it that taints our physical bravery as a nation with so much moral cowardice? Why is it that countless thousands will face shot and shell and wounds horrible beyond imagining with quiet heroism, and will yet shrink from the display of moral courage required to tell their rulers that, until the poorest child of England has its rights and its chance, they have failed in their duty, and that they must put the national house in order? I would wager that a majority, a large majority of both Houses of Parliament would be prepared to admit in private conversation all the claims I have put forward on behalf of the little ones, and that they would in public find a score of excuses for not pressing them. The most frequent excuse will of course be that after this war we shall lack the means. But I protest that whatever the date of peace, if it be a peace that meets our hopes, we shall be in a state in which we could find the means for at least another year of war if need be. Who will deny that it is better to create, cherish, and equip life than to devote our vast resources to its destruction? Equality, liberty, and fraternity are the first-fruits of liberal education, the fine flower of progress. The war found our wealth accumulating and our people deteriorating, so slowly to be sure that they were able to pull themselves together and appeal with certainty to the favourable verdict of world history, but yet deteriorating. Slums, prostitution, crime, insanity, drink, irresponsible wealth, all these evils were beginning to fester in the body politic, and war has applied the surgeon's knife to the open sore. Is peace to see it extirpated or allowed to grow again? I think in all honesty and sincerity that our treatment of the children will decide. If we will learn from our neighbours on the continent and our kinsmen across the Atlantic we may renew our strength. We may even justify the sacrifice of those who by reason of their love of England will never return to us.

There is another and a sacred ground for this appeal. Let us remember the nameless dead, those whose heroism is expressed in part of a crowded line of small print, who had nothing but their lives to offer to their country, who had no chance in life and who when the bands of the body were breaking gave their last anxious thoughts to little ones doomed under our harsh system of social life to drift where and how they can. Who among those they died to leave in security and a sufficiency of the world's goods would come forward and say, "In spite of all these dead men did for me I will oppose a measure that will give their children useful and honourable lives, because what is left to me of life will be passed without some luxuries I have enjoyed hitherto?" I venture to say there are none who would put this sentiment in words. Yet there are thousands, tens of thousands whose deeds will say it for them, not because they are utterly selfish, callous, or hard-hearted, but because they lack the saving grace of imagination. The most of the evil that disfigures the earth is due to this inability to see beyond our own needs. In the labour, the upheaval, the expense of a movement needed to equip the generation that will so soon succeed our own, we overlook the salient truth that it is no more than the fulfilment of a solemn duty, a pledge that binds us to the dead though it was never given. For who will suggest that the poor men, the bulk of those who fought and died for England, faced their fate to maintain the slum and the gin palace and the labour of the poor prostitute who sells her body that she may eat to live, or drink to forget how she is living? Surely they died for the faith that was in them, with some dim fore-knowledge of happier days for those they left behind. We are the executors of their unwritten testament. If, as so many believe, there is some form of consciousness in the unknown world of which they are the sudden denizens, will they not be looking even now to see if we whose debt is so great have determined to pay it? And what better faith can we keep than by giving to the lives they have left behind the simple rights that were denied to them? Every rich man, every member of the comfortable classes claims these benefits for his children, and if the war has given birth to a true spirit of brotherhood, the children of the poor cannot be forgotten. They lack the means, we have them. From this simple truth and the consequent, inexorable duty there is no escape with a clean conscience.

XIX

THE PRUSSIAN IN OUR MIDST

WAR throws a blinding light upon the strength and the weakness of nations, and in England we may claim that we have faced the light without any revelations of which we need feel ashamed. Our mistakes have been rather of temperament than character, and whether in mustering our millions on the voluntary system or surrendering our hard-won liberties to an authority that has shown no sign of suffering from wisdom in excess, or giving fully and freely of our resources to the national cause, we may claim to have shown in our collective capacity a generous response to the most varied and unexpected demands. Incidentally we have discovered in our midst a body of men, happily small in number, and not too significant in position, who would fain embody in our national life the worst vices that we are said to be fighting in the one foe that counts. These men, whose political sagacity exists in inverse ratio to their prejudices, are ever prompting the worst elements in our rulers and threatening and intriguing against the others.

To them war is no frightful necessity imposed upon a free and peaceful people, but a providential opportunity for taking occasion by the hand; the voice is the voice of Prussia, but the hands are English hands.

Our Prussians have always been in evidence, but, while the government of the empire was trusted to their friends, they were content to be quietly active. It is now nearly ten years since a Liberal Government came into power, and with the advent of Radical legislation our Prussians—they call them Tories over here—became active.

When taxation threatened their superfluous wealth, they called heaven and earth to witness that such an outrage had no sanction. When the House of Lords, long the supreme force of obstruction, was threatened they grew frantic, and at many a well-spread board declared themselves ready to dine—I mean die—in the last ditch before submitting to the indignity of democratic government.

When Home Rule was on the tapis they declared for revolution and civil war, and it needed Armageddon to burst the bladder of Sir Edward Carson's threats. In justice be it said that when the tocsin sounded the Tories responded to the nation's need, and forgot for a time their ineffective selves.

But as soon as the gravity of the task was revealed they decided that the authorities were useless without their judgment in aid. Cabal succeeded criticism, plots of exquisite silliness were hatched, matched, and dispatched. Then came the call for more soldiers, and our Prussians turned Conscriptionists.

The suggestion that conscription of men should be associated with conscription of wealth was dismissed as an impertinence, it sufficed if all that others possess were sacrificed for the State. Our Prussians talked incessantly of men and duty, but where finance was concerned they were content to warn the worker not to squander his extra wages earned by unremitting labour during a week seven days long. They saw with clear vision the iniquity of depriving the capitalist of half the wealth he is amassing as a result of the bloodiest war in history, and have protested almost in unison against the decree. They forgot with amazing ease that conscription is the force that has set the Prussian Jack-boot above all law human and divine; they clamoured for it here, doubtless with an eye upon the possibilities of coercing in days to come a proletariat of toilers forced to live under military law in time of peace. Disguised as patriots they thundered from a hundred platforms, they thumped a thousand tubs, while their hirelings in the Press wrote stodgily in admiration and support, pointing out that certain hard-jawed, soulless politicians would alone avail to save England from itself. As though England would endure to-day the undiluted political opinions of a Carson, a Milner, a Halsbury, or a Walter Long. Excellent men, no doubt, but never in their lives less than half a century behind the times.

Politicians and papers were aided by the truth that even the voluntary system has its flaws and hardships, its inequalities and petty tyrannies, and the Prussian remedy for the whip of voluntary service is the scorpion of conscription.

Those who do not agree with our Prussians are traitors to the height, although if our Prussians are patriots Dr. Johnson's definition of patriotism becomes dangerously true.

The question of peace discussion has been the latest consideration of these gentry. Personally I have no use for peace until we have won our victory or suffered our defeat. I believe we shall win, and that our first duties as victors will be to take whatever steps are needed to give peace permanence.

But I cannot follow our Prussians over one yard of their mile-long way. They would impose the methods of Berlin and Vienna upon all who dare to have opinions of their own, they would

repress individuality, they would out Herod the
Herods of the censorship who daily murder so much
childishness, they would in fact reduce free men
to the level of the citizens who serve their rulers
for "cannon fodder."

In one of the reactionary dailies written by Tories for Tories I have been reading with infinite
disgust a tribute of admiration to the "Stern Methods" of the Central Empires in dealing with "War
Cranks," *i.e.* with people whose sense of what they,
rightly or wrongly, believe to be truth is so strong
that they will sacrifice position, even life, to tell
the truth when they see it. "Hungarians," writes
our Prussian, "who were only suspected of not
approving of the war were interned or publicly
shot." Such a policy has more to justify it "than
have the liberties which are accorded to certain
sects who with their ideas form an insignificant, and
almost negligible minority." These sentiments are
even worse than the English used to express them.
One Hungarian publicist, M. Pazmaudy, aged
sixty-nine, went to prison for three months for
writing an unpublished letter to a newspaper in
which he denounced the war as wholesale murder.
A teacher who pointed out to his class that war
is the fruit of rulers' jealousy rather than of the
people's animosities, a statement that is probably
true of nine-tenths of the war recorded by his-

tory, was condemned to three years' hard labour. Our anonymous Prussian rejoices in these barbarities, and a paper supposed to represent the educated classes of England is not ashamed to print this revelation of an unsound or distorted mind.

In the early days of the war, Bernard Shaw reminded us that we, too, have our Junkers, and his statement has been proved up to the hilt. Our soldiers and sailors are fighting the Prussians abroad, and it is the duty of those of us who cannot help beyond England's boundaries, to fight the Prussians at home, for it is abundantly clear that we have them in our midst, those who are working night and day to give us Militarism, Absolutism, and every form of Central European slavery under another name. They desire an England of conscript workmen, they seek the destruction of Trade Unionism, and the abolition of socialism, though it is only by adopting that dread creed that the Government contrived to save our credit and to feed us. They wish to destroy the German militarism, and what it stands for, but only to take over the whole business, lock, stock, and barrel as a going concern. The truth is that the Tories can no more change their skin than the leopard his spots.

It is to them the ideal, merely the ideal, in the wrong hands. They see beyond the horizon of war the dawning of a democratic era that shall destroy privilege, and make our national freedom greater than it has ever been, and the prospect is more bitter to them than defeat. So while our men, so recently civilians, are proving the strength and resources of comparative freedom—what has been done is as little with what still remains to be done —our Prussians are putting forward all manner of chains for unfettered limbs, and are declaring that without them nothing can save the Empire. It is pleasant to reflect that after this war comes to its appointed close the vigorous democracies of Canada and Australia that have followed the United States along the road of political freedom will be finding representatives at the Council Board of Empire, and that they will be alert and vigorous to put an end to the machinations of our Prussians whose attack upon liberty will not readily be forgotten. When we attempt to measure the sacrifices that have been made in freedom's name since August, 1914, when we remember the spirit that has led men contentedly into the jaws of death, when we understand what our fighters have fought for, there is an indescribable sense of loathing for the men who, secure in England, are plotting to transfer Prussian principles across the North Sea. Their failure to achieve anything commensurate with the villainy of the attempt is neither palliation nor excuse.

Every one who has studied social conditions knows that our national ability to pit the unprepared British Empire against Germany armed to the teeth, has been due to the fact that our Empire holds millions who believe from the bottom of their hearts that it is worth living in and dying for. What would the Prussians make of our Empire if they were allowed to direct it? A happy hunting-ground for Junkers and a hell upon Earth for free men is the very best that they could accomplish.

Political insight, democratic foresight, prevision of the inevitable march of events, all these gifts are denied them. They have no sympathy with any freedom that could exist beyond the realms of the privileged classes, they are too blind to see the writing on the wall that tells them they have been found wanting.

This war has witnessed plenty of mistakes, some trivial, some serious; it has witnessed the birth of a certain number of oppressive and retrograde measures, and the death of national liberties of which we look with hope, even with certainty for the joyful resurrection.

Whatever has been bad, retrograde, or dangerous to democracy has won the unstinted approval of our Prussians; every other act of our rulers they have condemned.

XX

BEFORE the war, I heard some shrewd feminists say that the frivolity associated with the life of women at the time when they have ceased to be girls and have "come out," is a matter of environment rather than choice. They went so far as to assert that if a worthier goal were offered, a majority would seek it without a moment's hesitation. For all my sympathy with feminism, despite my heartfelt conviction that man needs woman's help in the task of administering the world that lies beyond the home, I had doubts, grave doubts. I thought that those who said these things had gone a little beyond their brief, and I remembered the French aphorism, *"la jeunesse n'a qu'un jour."* It seemed to me that an innate knowledge of the time-limit was the foundation of frivolity, and here, perhaps, I was looking back thirty years or more to the radiant season of my own *début*, and was remembering how the girls who became matrons were expected to play the rest of their part in the life symphony on muted strings. True it is that I helped to post-date the passing of the girl and the coming of the matron, but in those feverish times we all thought that the race was to the swift.

It may be that this conviction coloured my views; I believed that for the vast majority of young girls with prospects of a good time, there would be no pleasure in serious endeavour of any kind: that a sense of responsibility could not precede the State recognition of women and a sweeping measure of educational reform. As recently as the summer season of 1914, I found the new players feverishly excited by the old, old game, and pleasure instead of losing its savour seemed to have widened its boundaries and assumed shapes more fantastic than ever. I heard girls who were standing on the threshold of their career prattling of the joys to come as though life did not compass within its horizon one solitary sorrow or disappointment. Women of experience are, I think, stirred by these enthusiasms in their sisters or daughters, or young friends: they have learned a part of life's lesson, and know glad memories for an inalienable possession. It follows that they rejoice to see those who are near and dear to them treading the primrose path in the spring of their years, realising that when they look over the old road in the autumn days, their memory will help to gladden it with even fairer blossoms. If we know youth for the season of mental intoxication, we are not the less grateful to the gods who grant it to one and all, and if we are quite honest with ourselves we have been rather a little sorry for the girls who are serious before their time. But, while so many happy children, for after all they were little more, were bringing their healthy appetite to the banquet of life, "dawn was at hand to strike the loud feast dumb."

The effect of the upheaval upon the girls who had been presented in 1914, or would in the ordinary course of events have made their *début* since, has been startling, and it has taught me that not only are the working classes sound at the core—I never doubted this—but the leisured classes are in no whit inferior. Only an insignificant minority pursue pleasure at any price, and find in the horrors of our time a medium for publicity or dissipation. Over the not inconsiderable circle that I have the opportunity of observing there came, in the vast majority of cases, a startling change. The opportunities for frivolity under the rose were accepted only by a few who are constitutionally and irretrievably decadent, or actually vicious. The others passed pleasure by, sought duty wherever it was to be found, and became supremely happy in its pursuit. They taught me to realise that my feminist friends were right, and that environment

which could have moulded their plastic natures in
one mould, had no trouble in moulding them in another.

To do full justice to the fortunately circum-
stanced girls of England, for I take it that what
is true of London and many country homes will
apply elsewhere, it is necessary to remember that
they have known less of the horrors of war than
their sisters of almost all belligerent countries.
Some, very few, have heard one or two bombs
dropped from air-ships, the rest have seen no more
than the wounded men who are sufficiently well to
be brought over to England. They cannot even
have visualised the full tragedy of the struggle as
French and Belgian girls must have done, and,
above all, they are seldom imaginative, but just as
they were prepared less than two years ago to enjoy as good a time as life could afford, they are
now committed to the hardest tasks within their
competence. What they have lost in pleasure, they
have gained in self-respect, and a sense of true citizenship; above all, they realise that they are of
signal use to the State in the hour of its exceed-
ing great need. Part of the *rôle* so long denied to
them they have assumed, not only without challenge, but with acclamation.

They have one additional advantage in their new
sphere: they have never known the pursuits of nor-

mal times. While the doors of the ball-room and all that lies beyond were still shut, the doors of the Temple of Janus were torn asunder. They have no regrets, they do not miss the flavour of what they have never tasted. Life is so full for them that if pleasure were within their grasp they would lack the leisure as well as the inclination to grasp it. The example of fathers, brothers, boy friends, is an unending stimulus; all those they love best are looking to them with a gratitude or admiration that no pursuit of pleasure could have evoked. They have realised the high tension of the hour, they have risen silently and unostentatiously to the heights. Such tragedy as has come into their lives —and the mourning that so many wear is eloquent beyond all speech—has increased   rather than diminished their labours; it has brought them nearer to the actuality of things. Where one hoped that all would gather roses many have gathered rue, but they have learned to know it by the older name, herb-of-grace. They wear it as they work, and it has become one of the symbols of the bond that binds those who serve with those who suffer.

I have seen the girls of whom I write labouring with deft yet unaccustomed hands in the canteens, undertaking in the hospitals the menial work that falls to those who are yet untrained, giving to pain longer hours than they would have given to pleasure in happy times. They bring to their tasks the subtle indefinite charm that is the gift of their hour and was intended for a setting so different. Is it a part of their reward that their lives should not lack a generous gift of high romance? I cannot recall in any season over which my memory has control so many engagements and marriages as there have been of late. The old huckstering conditions would seem to have passed, the girls are no longer weighing chances, the men are no longer calculating coldly. Each sees the other at best. The girl knows that the lad who has given all and risked all for his country must be sound at heart, and that his scars are honourable; the young man knows that he cannot go wrong in choosing a girl who has left pleasure for duty, who has found high ideals and pursues them. These unions coming about in hours of deepest uncertainty, when the bride of one month may be the widow of the next, are calculated to bring out what is best in both, for the natural affection is leavened by mutual respect. I have heard worldly minded parents grieve, some have brought their tales of woe to my utterly unsympathetic ear; I rejoice in these marriages, and believe they are of happiest augury for the State. Surely those who wed under these conditions may hope to live on the high plane of idealism longer than those whose unions have been dictated by what is mis-called prudence, while the fruits of unions consummated in such solemn hours when the future of Europe trembles in the balances of God, will be a source of strength in the years to come. They will surely not be like the offspring of exaggerated comfort or monstrous luxury.

It seems to me, reviewing the accomplishment of so many girls I know best, that war, for all its tragedy, may well leave the poor remains of our civilisation better than it was in the season of our opulence. Without regard to money or to good looks some of the best elements of the race have mated, each partner to the union understanding in fashion hitherto unimaginable not only that the Empire is worth the best we have to offer, but that one and all, regardless of the world's favours, are bringing their sacrifice. The minorities, noisy or silent, with which we must hereafter deal, the residue of profit-hunters and pleasure-seekers, pass almost out of mind as one sees the extraordinary transformation that war has wrought in a class that was supposed to be utterly deaf to any call save the call of amusement. That there have been larger tributes to the national cause is a commonplace, that there has been a more striking one I, at least, deny.

Who was the cynic who said that woman was the

last animal that man would civilise? I hope and believe he has not lived as long as his libel, and yet I could wish that somewhere in the realms reserved for liars he could be permitted to see a few at least of the sights that have gladdened and stimulated me in the past twelve months, ever since the women workers in the Empire's cause became fully representative of every class in the realm.

XXI

THE SOCIAL HORIZON

VERY early in the war, almost before the Expeditionary Force was under arms, the Government was forced by the grave urgency of the national case to apply the principles of socialism to certain outstanding problems. To name only one instance, we may mention the work of the railways. Socialists have always urged that the railroads should be taken over by Government in the national interest, and countless reams of paper have been wasted by individualists to demonstrate the impossibility. But needs grew paramount, and the Government, by a stroke of the pen, took the railroads into its inexpert keeping. Nothing has happened to make the country regret the change. The fashion in which our railways (with a few notable exceptions) are conducted is so utterly bad and so profoundly inefficient, that Government, in giving precedence to Government business, made them very little worse. Fares are a trifle higher, trains rather less frequent, carriages dirtier than heretofore, but Government's proper needs and unprac-

tised handling could do little or nothing to depress
the normal standard. As the war progressed, and
various common-sense measures were required to
deal with war profits, war contracts, and war crises
generally, it was recognised with something akin
to dismay by the hierarchy that lives behind the
times that in many instances socialism had anticipated common-sense. Then a strange thing happened. In a very unguarded moment, Mr. Runci-
man, that bright young man whose statesmanlike
qualities and keen sympathy with our poor ship-
owners have endeared him to a small minority at
least of English-speaking people, was heard to declare before a pained and startled House of Com-
mons that where Socialism was practical and met
the needs of the hour, he was prepared to adopt it.
In other words, he would not discard a useful measure because it was socialistic in origin or tendencies!
What magnanimity; what a sterling recognition of
a nation's needs!

Nobody perhaps quite knows what measure of
concession to hard truth was here intended, but as
a statement made by a President of the Board of
Trade, the utterance deserved more attention than
it received. Perhaps the Press Bureau asked newspapers to take no marked notice of a hard-worked
"statesman's" slip of the tongue. One would wager
that it did not pass altogether unrebuked by those

descendants of the wise men of Gotham, who would
rather see the Empire lost by party politicians than
saved by Socialists or Socialism.

It is a curious fact, and one that the historian
of the future will surely acknowledge, that Individualism has been discredited by the war, and that
the appeal of both our leaders and misleaders,
whatever the colour of their party-political opinions, has been to the principles underlying Socialism. Even in Russia, an autocracy, a land in which
the Tsar comes in the popular mind very near to
God, the appeal to the nation has been an appeal,
however unconsciously, to Socialism. The root
principle of Socialism lies in a great National Act.
The nation must work together for the national
good. So far has this idea developed that in the
last days of February, a reputed reactionary, M.
Markoff, rose in the Duma to implore the Government "to withdraw its shield from the old gang of
officials who look upon their country's adversities
merely as a favourable opportunity for increasing
their perquisites" (*Daily Telegraph*, Feb. 28th).
Here, under the pressure of giant circumstance,
we find an appeal made for the united action and
the national act. In Germany, as all our responsible, and not a little of the irresponsible, Press has
frankly admitted, the Socialist party is the only
one that has kept its head, and endeavoured in very

difficult circumstances to preserve ideals. The
Vorwarts, leading organ of German Socialism,
though it regards the war as an evil for which Germany was not responsible, has courageously opposed all the actions of the governing class that
have tended to lower the character of the German
people, and I have heard some of the best informed
students of European politics declare that, had Social Democracy been allowed another ten years of
peaceful development throughout the German Empire, no German ruler would have dared provoke
a war for the hegemony of Europe. They cannot
deny that Socialism, in its International aspect,
was making for the brotherhood of man. No other
force in national life was working with any approach to equal strength and sincerity along the
same road and in pursuit of the same goal.

Unfortunately, under the conditions that beset
and damn all Europe, the people have no voice in
the supreme decision of war. Their privilege is
to fight those with whom they have no quarrel.
Theirs, too, to sacrifice in appalling numbers their
fathers, husbands, brothers, and sons, to give up
their homes and savings, to acquiesce blindly in
every evil that marches in the wake of strife. Just
as the men ordered from the trenches to be mown
down by shot and shell are given or offered some
form of raw spirit to stimulate and even intoxicate

them, so before war is declared, Governments, through the medium of a docile Press, circulate the lies best calculated to make the imminent enormity appear inevitable and just. As soon as the declaration of war is made, the common patriotism of nations obscures every other issue. Men must fight for hearth and home, for fatherland and all that it implies. Primal necessity is speaking, and on every banner of every nation the ominous words "Væ victis" are inscribed. The people who make war and, somewhere out of Death's ample range direct it, understand the psychology of nations; their skill in all the arts of deception is unrivalled. Yet of all the lessons enforced by the war there is none that has come with greater force to all whose minds are not hermetically sealed than the lesson that Individualism has failed completely in the hour of the world's extremist need. The price we have paid for it within the compass of two brief years is the total loss of millions of lives, the future ineffectiveness of still more, the sheer, brutal waste of wealth more than sufficient to have solved all the economic troubles of Europe. Countless thinkers in all belligerent countries have been forced to the conclusion that Socialism is the only force capable of rendering what is left of Europe capable and adequate to the demands upon it. Great Britain, insular by act of God and the general tendency of the population, is fully prepared to accept Socialism as long as it is not called by that name, for such is the state of our mental development that we judge all political goods by their labels. In other countries, where social, political, and economic conditions are not merely discussed, but understood, where the people's representatives are required to have some minimum of knowledge in addition to birth, money, and influence, these concessions to popular ignorance and prejudice have been swept aside. The recognition of the necessity for sweeping changes is made without fear. Even in Germany, when Dr. Frank, the eminent Socialist, was reported killed, a statement was published to the effect that the Kaiser had expressed his regrets at the death of a man whose gifts would have helped the country in the days when schemes of reconstruction are under consideration.

This may have been no more than a sop to the social Democrats, of whom upwards of two millions have been called to the colours, but even if this be so, the sop is a significant one, and could not have been lightly given.

In stricken Belgium, the man who comes next to King Albert in sheer patriotic endeavour and in the gift of inspiring the nation to hold up its head under conditions hard for any of us to realise, is the famous Socialist leader, Emile Vandervelde.

He is not only at the head of the Belgian Ministry of War, but is King Albert's most trusted adviser; his gifts overshadow those of his equally devoted and patriotic colleagues. The thrill of horror and shame that ran through France when Jean Jaurés fell to the assassin's bullet in the opening days of war, was felt far beyond the French borders. Even in the tense excitement of that unhappy season, the French Government, after voting the murdered patriot a public funeral, posted in every Commune throughout the country its expression of horror and regret. To-day, a Socialist Prime Minister directs with rare skill and courage the fortunes of the Republic; the French National Council has not hesitated to summon to its ranks such an uncompromising foe of Individualism in whatever form as Jules Guesde. None, having eyes to see, ears to hear with, and even a modest gift of comprehension, can fail to gather from this the tendency of the great Power with which we are now so closely allied. Of all the European nations there is none in which the gift of political sagacity is so strongly marked as it is in France, none to which the gifts of political foresight and courage have been granted in equal measure. What Paris thinks to-day, London must be at least prepared to discuss in the very near future.

There is no secret about the cause of the action

that France and Belgium have taken of set purpose. The whole essence of a successful struggle is unity—unity of purpose, of feeling and of thought. The working classes, now as ever, are bearing in every country the bulk of the burden of war. Sane Governments must needs endeavour to secure for labour an adequate representation in their midst. Knowing that their proper interests are being subordinated, if at all, to the national cause, and not for private profit or exploitation, labour feels that it is secure, and will give all it has to give with a generosity that may be rivalled, but can never be excelled. The white flame of patriotism is only kept glowing if it is fed by the efforts of a whole community. This result will never be quite realised here in England until all interests are united in a Cabinet that stands just now for very little more than the propertied classes. I admit, Mr. Henderson, Mr. Brace, and Mr. Wardle, have all been given some office to placate the great Trade Unions from which so much is demanded to-day. But this is not enough. Our Cabinet of aged ostriches still hides its head in the bushes of precedent and prejudice, content to believe that what it does not wish to see can have no existence, and fortified in this strange method, that would be comic if it were not tragic, by all sections of the capitalistic Press. International Socialism is gathering its forces throughout Europe, and in the United States as well, to impose permanent peace on kings and other anachronisms. Thinking people in all the centres of civilisation agree that this war is sounding the knell of privilege. But England remains content to be ruled by lawyers, professional politicians, mid-Victorian relics, and doctrinaires. Socialism, the master force of the immediate future, is deliberately ignored. Well might Father Adderley (Canon the Honourable James Adderley, so beloved in the slums of Plaistow and Birmingham) deplore in his recently published memoirs, the absence from Parliament or from the Government itself, of H. M. Hyndman, the Nestor of English Socialism. The astonishing part of our national attitude towards this crisis is that the men who really guide and influence our public opinion, the live men of letters, are for the most part Socialists, and make no secret of their principles, nor have they ever hesitated to voice their suspicion of what Matthew Arnold called "the unelastic pedantry of theorising Liberalism." Does this Government think that all this teaching has fallen or is falling on deaf ears? Does it forget that it was the French Encyclopædists who made the French Revolution? They taught a discontented and unhappy people to think and the people did the rest. Our rulers have always moved respectfully behind the times, but, to do them what justice we may, be it remembered that they never expected to live through seasons that impel the times to move with giant and sudden strides.

Now, even in the latter days, all these things have come upon them. Will they, can they, rise to the height of the occasion?

XXII

IT is not without a certain significance that, while French and German soldiery were sacrificing themselves by their thousands to the Gods of War in and around the blood-stained village street of Douaumont, while our soldiers were holding on to the line of the Tigris, near whose source Russian forces were marching southward to the rescue, the Royal Commission appointed to investigate what is euphemistically called "Social Disease," issued its report. The coincidence from certain view-points is startling.

The report, definitely limited as to its scope, sober in its statement, and appalling in its revelation, is a solemn reminder to the world of civilised men that there are enemies equally deadly and more insidious than those with whom any belligerent is concerned. The victims of the diseases discussed probably outnumber, in Great Britain alone, all her defenders on sea and land. Four millions of our population, with power to add to their number, are at grips with a deadly enemy in various stages of its virulence; an enemy who will "visit the sins of the fathers upon the children to the third and fourth generation." Nay more, the Commissioners whose trained minds lend solid value to their every utterance, assure us that after a war an excessive incidence of disease is certain to occur, even in districts previously free. There are other significant comments. "Our evidence," they tell us, "tends to show that the communication of disease is frequently due to intoxicants, and there is no doubt that the growth of temperance among the population would help to bring about an amelioration. We are also conscious of the fact that overcrowded and insanitary dwellings contribute to the spread of disease, and from improvements in this direction we should expect some diminution of its prevalence."

Let us consider the full meaning of these vivid comments. When war is over, we shall celebrate the coming of peace throughout the length and breadth of these islands. Countless offerings will be laid before the altar of the brewer and the distiller; it will be almost dangerous to be an abstainer. For a time, at least, the barriers of restraint will be torn down. Something known as "good fellowship" will at once dictate and excuse an orgie. The discipline that weak minds require will be honoured in the breach rather than the observance, and "an excessive incidence of disease is certain to occur, even in districts previously free."

When a town is successfully invaded, and a soldiery, grown reckless after lying cheek by jowl with death flings his self-discipline, mercy, and restraint to the winds, the world that has not lost its reason is sick at heart. When peace is proclaimed, and the return to civil life is associated with a licence that outrages the living and damns the unborn, there is apparently no authority that can intervene, no public opinion capable of making itself felt. The living, and those upon whom the heaviest burden of life is to be imposed, are alike unprotected. Not only is this so, but the conditions that must make for their undoing are cultivated in the interests of those who flood the land with spirits and malt liquors. What if our slums help infection to spread? Are not slum-owners often men of repute, some of whom sit in the high seats of judgment and help to administer a world they are willing to degrade still further in the sacred name of rent? Do we not make a man a Peer if he can brew sufficient beer? The Commissioners know better than to plead for an England sober or an England adequately housed. Theirs not to presume to attack vested interests. They have dared greatly in pointing out what the slum and the gin palaces contribute to the spread of most loathsome diseases under heaven. There they must stop. They know their public. "Improvement in the social conditions and in the moral standard may be slow." They have realised what our modern political conditions stand for throughout Great Britain. They even admit that there may be no money for improvement; European civilisation, however inadequate to human needs, however imperfect and incomplete, can only be destroyed at heavy expense. The destruction demands the best life-blood of every belligerent nation and all available financial resources. What can be left to combat "social disease," cancer, consumption, drink, slums, and the other evils that destroy even more than war, but have nothing arresting or spectacular in their methods? The Commissioners plead, it would seem, with more of earnestness than hope.

Perhaps the most appalling side of "social disease" is due to its utter absence of respect for persons. We could wish in the interests of humanity as at present constituted that the germs could themselves be inoculated with genuine English snobbery, so that they would refrain from attacking "high personages." Apparently, germs are untutored things. They ignore class distinctions. They attack with equal impartiality the drunken soldier of a garrison town, the sailor set free, after a long voyage, in an evil seaport with

money burning holes in his pocket, and the crowned
head who, in the days of his indiscretion, lived as
lewdly as the soldier or sailor without the excuse
of either. The wages of sin is death. "Social
disease" affects the ordered function of the brain,
and when that brain is in the skull of one who con-
trols the destinies of Empire, the dread death-
wages must be paid by the rank and file of his
subjects. Nobody has dared yet to write fully
and freely of the influence of social disease upon
the decrees of European rulers. Though the hideous facts are known well enough in certain circles, they are hardly discussed. Perhaps the scandal is one from which the sharpest pen shrinks ap-
palled. Consider the *cercle privé* from which Europe's dynasts spring, the tendencies of upbring-
ing, the intermarriage, the temptation, the effect
upon narrow minds and exhausted stocks. The
light is beginning to shine upon thrones. The
world is beginning to ask why so much of madness
is manifest in the ranks of rulers, and whether in
the wide interests of humanity the breed is not of
more importance than the blood. At present the
question is asked *sotto voce,* the time is surely coming when it will ring through Europe. But for
the moment there is a still larger question at stake.

The publication of the Royal Commission's Report is a warning and a challenge to the democracy,

not only of Great Britain, but of the world. It tells them that the real, the enduring enemy, is not the German, the Briton, the Frenchman, or the Russian. The enemy is not on the battlefield, but in the homeland, in the street, perhaps in the house. He has invaded every country in Europe without exception. Battleships, heavy ordnance, elaborate trenches, are of no avail. Treaties of peace cannot be made effective until they are signed between a vigilant and victorious democracy on the one hand and a defeated, privileged class on the other.

The national resources required to meet a foul disease are taken from us to-day in measure beyond precedent to meet an expenditure for which the demand was created by kings and statesmen. There was no reference to the will of the people; until such time as that will could be neither logical nor effective. The world's working men, decimated to satisfy the ambitions of their misrulers, must return in greatly diminished numbers and with lives crippled and wasted by the million, to find the old enemies at their gate and the worst and ugliest of these enemies prepared to take advantage of peace by waging more deadly war. And those who will administer their shattered dynasties will include members of families that are notoriously tainted by "social disease." Surely viler prospect were hard to find.

Yet there is not under heaven an evil for which there is no remedy. If the people sacrificed to armament makers, diplomats, and dynasts will join hands across the world they can overcome the enemies without and within. Their strength, if they will but put it forward, is irresistible, far greater than they know. They should have no more illusions. They are many; those who exploit them are few. Before the war the great international movement was growing. A series of ultimatums, of frenzied calls to patriotism, racial prejudice and fear, frosted the ripening blossoms, but could not reach the root that lies deep down in the heart of suffering humanity. Internationalism will rise again. Those who have a finger upon the pulse of the workers the world over, know that the life forces, depressed for a time, are giving a growing vigour to the beat. Already they see the rulers of the world deploring the catastrophe that they brought about, becoming conscious that their hands drip blood. Already they see that normal evils are not merely remaining unabated but are actually growing, that a world returned to sanity and humility will find more vileness to combat and fewer means to its aid. It will look for a lead.

That is why there is so much reason to hope that the United States will not be drawn into war. There, the workers of Europe are already beginning to look for guidance, direction, help, and actual co-operation in the ultimate struggle for freedom, that when war is over they may combat the yet worse evils around them. Our thoughts turn to the New World, redeemed from kings and popes and the tragic remains of feudalism, and, largely on that account, at peace. Consider the vile, naked truth that we in England may lack the means adequately to conquer the "social disease," the white scourge, the slum problem, and other shames of man's own making because our national resources are being sacrificed to such destruction as sun, moon, and stars have never looked upon since first they lit the earth.

Our rulers, our statesmen, our parliaments, our laws alike, have failed us. Judge them by their fruits, as hereafter surely they must be judged. There is nothing left between Europe and the abyss but the solidarity of the working classes, the spread of democracy, the overthrow of every effete institution that exists for no better reason than that it has been allowed to exist so long. We, the Internationalists, look to the United States, that island of sanity set in a raging sea of madness. We look to it for light and leading, for encouragement and support. It is the only great power left to read the lessons of world-war without prejudice. I would like the terrible indictment penned against

our modern civilisation by the Royal Commission
to be read by every thinking American of whose
political faith democracy is the vital essence.*

> "This is that Blossom on our human tree
> Which opens once in many myriad years
> But opened, fills the world with Wisdom's scent
> And Love's dropped honey."

---

* I would like it studied in the red light of war, that our
cousins oversea with their generous instincts, quick judgment
and resourceful minds may be stimulated to assist the workers
of all nations when once this terrible chapter of our life is
closed. United action will make impossible in the future all
wars save that which is waged against disease, privilege, and
ineffectiveness.

XXIII

HOW I WOULD WORK FOR PEACE

FOR a long time past, ever since it was realised that the countless campaigns to which we are committed would be long in following their appointed course, costly in progress and revolting in detail, all manner of people have come forward to explain that they have mastered the causes and the cure of war. Belligerent and neutral countries alike have put forward their panaceas, and Great Britain has held some particularly active groups, perhaps because, while strife fills her horizon, only Zeppelins have succeeded in bringing the actualities home to those who are not serving. Then, too, we have always had in the country a number of men and women who believe honestly that war is a madness and crime, that their contention can be proved by argument, and that because they imagine war does not really benefit anybody, nobody really wants war.

There are others who do not go quite so far as this, being content to saddle policies or individuals with the responsibility. Secret diplomacy is, we are assured, a fruitful source of wars, and we are invited to place our cards on the table, and instruct our diplomats to tell the truth, the whole truth, and nothing but the truth. Out of these theories are born societies like the Union of Democratic Control, and many unnecessary speeches by people who are apt to confuse martyrdom and unpopularity.

War gives rise to optimists, like Mr. Henry Ford, who, quite oblivious to gibes and sneers, charters a steamer and proceeds to Europe, that he may call upon belligerents to cease their quarrels, because even from the distant city of Detroit, he can see how foolishly they are behaving.

It may be easy to laugh or to sneer at these manifestations. I find it impossible to do either. In every one of these efforts, great or small, notable or ludicrous, something of the spirit that is helping the world to progress is made manifest. If men and women who have little in life except the respect of their circle, deliberately sacrifice that precious asset for the sake of saying what they believe to be the truth, they are worthy of regard, and let us remember that most of us are amongst those who would rather be stoned than laughed at.

If I have criticism for panaceas that are to rid the nation of war as patent medicine-vendors offer to rid the individual of disease, if I look a little askance at all schemes of international betterment by will of the people, it is because all equality of reasoning power, all movement towards higher things, is conditioned by education.

We are very much like our fruit-trees. If you plant one hundred trees of equally good appearance and quality on a good soil, and you attend to fifty, and leave the other fifty to look after themselves, what is going to happen? The trees that have clean soil round the roots, that are pruned and washed and shaped in the way they should go will yield abundantly, look well, and live long; the others will be uncertain in their growth, unattractive in aspect, and liable to fail or become diseased.

In England we pay scant heed to the prosperity of the race, we are far more concerned with the prosperity of the race-course. We have been taught to care less for the well-being of the public than of the publican.

I do not write in any bitterness of spirit, but I remember how long, and successfully the race-course struggled against the war, how definitely Mr. Lloyd George's attempt to end the drink traffic was defeated by the "trade," and how, on the other hand, certain alleged economies in our schools, designed to save a few pounds at the cost of efficiency, have been accepted with hardly a protest.

If we wish to raise another generation that may benefit by the lessons we have learned and paid so dearly for, we must educate it, and education must be recognised as a necessity, something as necessary to us as the bread we eat, and more important than professional politicians, public-houses, race-courses, theatres, and motor-cars; more vital to our welfare than all the amusements of the rich and the poor put together.

Without education, the best ideas, the highest ideals must be lost and, as things are here, so they are elsewhere. In Europe the only belligerent countries that have developed education all over their territory are France and Germany. In some of the other countries, the schoolmaster does not cover a tithe of the domain, and rulers do not wish to see the area of activity enlarged, partly because they understand it is easier to deceive, divide, and rule the ignorant, and partly because they know that the rank and file will not be able to keep pace with the enlightened intelligences to which the most restless elements in the State will be attracted. Autocratic rule cannot endure indefinitely in countries where the proletariat has been to school, even military domination might in time be questioned.

But what bearing has this upon world war? you may ask, and I reply that it has a considerable bearing upon the whole question, because the great majority of those who ensue peace are preaching just now to the converted.

Those who make the next war may be despotic or unconstitutional rulers, if Europe is of a mind to endure such people after this, but they will depend largely upon the uneducated classes, or upon an iron discipline that makes every man a slave of him who represents the State. Education is the one reliable antidote to absolute monarchy, and despite its complete failure in July and August, 1914, I am still inclined to have faith in the International. It failed then, for each belligerent country called out that it was in danger, and in that hour when the social democracy might have saved Europe from the loss of millions of promising lives, the savings of one generation and the progress of two, it failed. But nobody will recognise more completely than the social democrat the price of failure; he will see that democracy must be in future as independent of boundaries as is art or science.

I believe that scores of men and women have the right peace methods, that there are many plans by which peace might be assured to the world, but no one of these can possibly become effective unless it can appeal to the men who constitute the rank and file of the world's armies, and to their wives and sweethearts.

The only other way out of the tangle is for victory to fall upon the side of those who are really concerned to keep the peace, and there is more than a little danger in this, for those who are concerned only with peace are apt to forget war altogether—to neglect necessary precautions, cut down reasonable expenditure, and in short, to give the war-loving, but weaker races, a chance of challenging peace afresh. A union of the world's democracies is the cure for war, and this union is not possible until a certain standard of education has been reached by one and all. Only then will the man to whom fighting is the breath of life understand that he must control his murderous instincts òr perish by them.

This war cost many years of preparation, part of it secret, and it is hard to see that peace can be more than a state of neutrality enforced by poverty and exhaustion. To make it abiding will need something more than the skill and cunning of diplomats, it will require the consent of the people themselves, and this they will give when they have knowledge, and not before.

Educate! Use all the modern developments of our civilisation to that end. Let every child in Europe be taught to read and be supplied with books; let every new railway line be hailed as an ambassador of peace. Let interchange of visits be arranged between the workers of all countries, so that they may learn that antagonisms belong to their rulers and not to them.* It would be a fine thing to have a panacea that acted as quickly as quack medicines claim to act, but we all know that such cures do not exist. You cannot accomplish in a few months the work that thousands of years have left unfinished. After all that has been said, let us remember that war has been allowed to be the rule of life for countless generations. We in England have hardly suffered, the United States have kept free from actual invasion, but nearly all the other great Powers have known its horrors within the comparatively brief period of our lifetime.

On the Continent, war is one of the incidents of normal life. Men are trained to take part in it as a completion of their education, women are encouraged to applaud it as the source of all honours and distinction. England and America, the two least threatened countries, would hardly appear in a good light as peace propagandists on the Continent, for war is received in a certain false perspective there. Thousands glory in the thoughts of a campaign, proud to have taken part in one as our grandfathers were to empty two or three bottles at a sitting. This false perspective is the greatest danger we have to face in educating the people: it

---

* A schoolmaster in Austria for saying as much as this was sentenced to several years' hard labour.

must be destroyed before war will be seen as the thing it is.

Human nature being hard to move, the work must progress slowly, but it is not the less worth undertaking on that account. Sane peace propaganda, accompanied by encouragement of physical fitness and explanation of the significance of life, need offend none, and will benefit all.

The real facts of war must be within reach of everybody, the camera should preserve the records of trench, battlefield, and sacked town. Every city should engrave its list of dead where all may read, and in the cities that have suffered from invasion the full details of the horror should be preserved. The taxation that will grip Europe for many a year to come should always be associated with its prime cause, and every device should be sought to impress upon the children who will now be growing up into an impoverished world, the folly and helplessness of their parents who were unable to keep what they had inherited, whether of freedom or worldly wealth.

We who are middle-aged will be hardly called upon to see war again, the generation captured in its prime between the summers of 1914 and 1916, will have been ruined, the rule of the world will wait upon those who are just leaving school.

Here the propagandists must work, and as there

is hardly a big family in belligerent Europe that has not contributed life or fortune in some degree, the foundation for the work will stand prepared.

If I were asked how to develop sane peace propaganda, I would call upon those who have gone through the war to tell the full story to those who have remained behind. All should unite to this end when war is over. Not only should the Englishman tell of frozen trenches and waterless deserts, but Germans and Austrians should tell of the retreat in Galicia and the advance to the marshes of Poland and Russia. The Servian retreat to Albania and the nameless horrors of Armenia should be recorded by survivors, women for choice, and men of all belligerent countries should speak of the horrors of the man-of-war that sinks blazing into the depths.

The camera has a tale to tell of devastated country-side and ruined city, of all the havoc and waste of war. Let that tale be told.

Let the maimed, the crippled, the blind, the physically useless, come forward—our eyes will learn their lesson.

Let the Churches speak, not at the bidding of authority, but in response to the plea of humanity.

Let War, divorced from the physical training incumbent upon men and women alike, take its place by the side of cancer, cholera, and plague.

Let the authorities tell us the loss of all communities in material wealth, and the eugenist speak of the blow to civilisation.

Let all the accumulated facts be on record in every public library in the world, and let them be available even to the illiterate.

Here, then, when the greatest of world-tragedies draws to its appointed close, is the means I would choose to render its repetition impossible, believing as I do that ignorance is the root from which all evil springs.

XXIV

LORD FRENCH

My first meeting with Field-Marshal Viscount French, so long Commander-in-Chief of the "contemptible little army" that has made history, dates back to the South African War. My latest meeting with him before he returned from France, was in August, 1914. On each occasion he was on the point of leaving for the front.

In the wide space that separates the Boer War from the great international conflict, we met very often; he was frequently our guest, and we visited him at Government House, Aldershot. I have had many opportunities of hearing his views of the world problem that confronts us now, for he had seen it coming nearer and nearer, and had laboured night and day to meet it. Other men had doubts; he found no room for any.

It was at Claridge's Hotel in town that we met during the Boer War. My eldest son, Guy, had then arrived at the ripe age of seventeen, and still at Eton, had sold all his personal effects, including his fur coat and jewellery given him by family and friends, to provide himself with the means of getting to the front and equipping himself when there. We only learned his intentions when it was too late to stop them, and I do not think that either my husband or myself was really anxious to keep him from serving his country. The only difficulty was to find him something useful to do, and Sir John French offered to take him on his staff as galloper.

I recall Lord French as I saw him at Claridge's—firm-mouthed, curt in manner, briefly incisive in speech, saying no more than was absolutely necessary, and looking at me with the curious glance that bespeaks the man of action who dreams and sees visions. A strong, resolute figure, with an iron will behind it, a human war machine in perfect order—that was my first impression.

Many of my soldier friends were with him in South Africa, where his gifts as a cavalry leader roused enthusiasm. Writing home from the front, they told me he had but one fault as a commanding officer—he could not realise that horses do not respond as readily as soldiers to human emotions. He could overdrive his men, and they did their utmost for him, as they did for another martinet, the late General Gatacre, because in each case they had implicit belief in their leader's direction and unbounded faith in his skill, but he over-worked his horses, and kept the remount department in despair.

He came back to England wearing all the laurels of a successful general, and I met him several times in town. "The dust of praise that is blown everywhere" was no more to John French than any other dust. He brushed it sharply away, and devoted all his leisure to considering the problems of the inevitable struggle with Germany. He believed then, with that curious gift of divination, that it must come, and he came near to fixing the date, for many years have passed since he assured me that it would not be later than 1915.

When the Entente Cordiale was in the air and there was a chance that Great Britain and France would work side by side, he was delighted. Such an arrangement was for him an ideal one, and he was, I may say, one of the first, if not the very first, of our leading military men who showed a full appreciation of its value. Unfortunately, though a well-educated and, in a strictly professional sense, a deeply read man, he had no knowledge of the French language, and he could not rest until that defect was remedied. So in the Summer of 1906— I think this was the year—he settled in the little village of La Boulé, near Rouen, and lived for three months in absolute retirement, mastering the language. He would not claim to have acquired the Parisian accent, but he can at least speak fluently.

We were motoring through France that summer

and stayed in the little hotel he had chosen for his headquarters. He was extremely anxious to take me on a motor tour over the scene of Napoleon's last campaign, an ambition of long standing only now possible of fulfilment. We came very near to going with him, but unfortunately, something intervened. Even Lord French cannot make war anything but unspeakably horrible to me, but I am yet free to confess that his vast knowledge and soul-deep convictions make it fearfully interesting.

We could not manage the motor tour, which would have covered Waterloo, but later, when in Paris, I was able to put his views before the then Premier, M. Clemenceau, whom I knew well. I had a very long and intimate conversation about the Entente with the "Tiger," as they called him in France, and I remember how he wheeled round in his chair and said to me in the frank, outspoken way that his opponents hate and fear, "Lady Warwick, the Entente is of no use to us unless your country can put 400,000 soldiers into France in the hour of need." I may remark that the French army was not then in its present state of efficiency.

I pointed out that I was not in the confidence of our War Office, and that his application should be made to other quarters, and went on to ask him to meet General French to talk over the matters in question. "I'll do that with pleasure," said M.

Clemenceau. "I regard your General French as one of the few soldiers who understand military problems from their roots upwards." So the two men met, and I think they liked and respected one another.

I remember reporting the gist of their conversation in a long letter to King Edward, who in his reply told me his interest in the military side of the Entente had been greatly strengthened. In the following year several of the leading generals of France were invited over to attend the military manoeuvres and were the guests of Sir John and Lady French at Government House, Aldershot. I was asked to meet them, and heard at first hand the discussion of many difficulties that are staring us in the face as I write. I do not think I have ever had more occasion to be glad that I was taught some foreign languages properly.

On his return to England Sir John French divided his work into sections. First and foremost came the German question, for he knew perfectly well, in the light of the ample information that came to him, how, sooner or later, Germany would fling down the gauntlet, perhaps before Europe, certainly before Great Britain. His other task was concerned with the possible invasion of India by Russia. In early days he had seen service in India, and I have by me now a copy of his own plans for the defence of our great empire there.

King Edward took Lord French with him when he went to meet the Czar at Réval, and this visit, at which the foundation of Anglo-Russian good-fellowship was laid, had a most reassuring effect upon his mind. Thereafter he devoted himself whole heartedly to the study of the Anglo-German danger.

Taking for his motto the well-known maxim that it is allowable to learn even from an enemy—he adapted what he thought was best from the German methods, and it is well known that he and his close and trusted friend, Sir Douglas Haig, in making the British Army the perfect machine that it is, bore well in mind the lessons to be gathered from the German manœuvres.

He objected strongly to the German close formation, holding it wasteful and unwise. He had grafted South African experience on his stock of tactical knowledge, and if the drilling of our men was terribly hard, he and Sir Douglas found the ripe fruits of it in that wonderful retreat from Mons and in the battles round Ypres. For German thoroughness he had a generous and unstinted admiration. Prejudice can find no place in his mind.

His prevision of the course of the present campaign startles me as I recall it now. He told me years ago much that has happened since the greatest world struggle of history began.

A born soldier, he is merciless to the inefficient. He broke a high officer, who was also a personal friend, because that officer made a bad blunder. Private considerations were swept aside, as they always are with him. He spares nobody, least of all himself, but his men love him almost as much as they trust him, and he watches over their proper comforts with a jealous eye. They are the component parts of the war machine, and must be at their best.

Lord French has not much in common with his gifted sister, Mrs. Despard, who was prominently before the public when the suffrage question came near to rivalling Home Rule in its claim on public attention, for Mrs. Despard's life is one of self-sacrifice to lighten the sorrows of others. But to one well acquainted with brother and sister, there are the qualities of calm resolution in the face of danger and of commanding will to be associated with each.

I do not think he reads much, save books dealing with military questions. He does not hunt or shoot, or play polo or, indeed, acknowledge any form of sport. He stands professionally as far apart from the ordinary mundane interests of life as any professor in the cloistered peace of an old

university town, and yet he is full to the brim of
vitalising enthusiasms not to be overlooked by his
friends because they are controlled.

He lives in his profession and breathes the very
air of it; soldiering claims his every thought, and
yet he is in no aspect the "beau sabreur" of the
Ouida novels. If you were to drive with him
through the most exquisite landscape, his mind's
eye would at once select the salient points of attack and defence, he would grasp every military
possibility of what lay before him, but the surrounding beauty would pass him by. Sometimes
we have talked of war. "I hate war as much as
you do," he has said to me more than once,
"but——" There it ends, and he is looking with
far-seeing eyes at encounters yet to be.

In the conventional sense he has no religion, and
yet I regard him as one of the most religious men
I know. His views of the hereafter are clear; he
is confidently assured of the soul's survival, its re-
incarnation, the fulfilment of its ambitions. He
is an idealist, an enthusiast, a man who could not
act dishonestly if he tried, faithful to the bitter end
to those in whom he trusts.

Much of the recent gossip in London has endeavoured to suggest that he has been a party to
the intrigues of others. I venture to say that nobody who understands Lord French could make

such a foolish mistake. The personal interests and trickery of small natures have no meaning for him. First and last and all the time he is a soldier, probably the one soldier who could have overcome the enormous difficulties by which he has been faced. He is the type of the leader of men, an example of the power of concentration driving a single purpose to its end. I think Frederick the Great would have made much of him and that his chief hero in a military sense, the first Napoleon, would have kept him by his side.

He has been sorely tried. It is to be hoped that Sir Douglas Haig, who in a military sense is his creation, will realise his teacher's dreams and ambitions.

XXV

LORD HALDANE: SOME RECOLLECTIONS AND AN ESTIMATE

IN the library this morning I came by chance upon a book that should not have been there—a "Life of Lassalle" that Lord Haldane lent me some years ago, and which I had forgotten to return. It chanced that within the hour I had thrown aside in disgust the Tory daily paper that held a vulgar and rancorous attack upon the Ex-War Minister. Perhaps it was the coincidence that set me thinking.

My mind travelled back to the day not so many years ago—King Edward had lately ascended the throne—when I met Lord Haldane for the first time. It was at Dalmeny, Lord Rosebery's home on the Firth of Forth. I forget who was of the party, at least I can remember only Winston Churchill, then coming under our host's political influence. My first recollection of Mr. Haldane as he was in those days was meeting him in the Library. He was busy arranging his host's treasures to the best advantage and was very little concerned with the house party's social side. He would

appear at table, create an immediate impression
by reason of his illuminating conversation, and, the
meal taken, would slip back again to his beloved
books. I carried away from Dalmeny the impression of one of the most interesting men I had ever
met—a man with massive head, twinkling eye and
witty speech that stimulated all and hurt none.
He was that *rara avis* a lawyer without guile, a
philosopher untainted by the Courts. We met
again, and again I was immensely attracted by his
personality. In the world we met in, men and
women were seeking success of some sort all the
time. Wealth, prestige, political power, social influence, whatever our weakness it rose to the surface like a cork. Of all these things Mr. Haldane
seemed supremely unconscious, he swam through
the social waters like a kindly triton among min-
nows. Even in those days he had long been a de-
vout student and an ardent admirer of what was
best in Germany, and I think it was because I too
was interested in the marvellous progress of that
Empire that we found something in common. And
he lent me the "Life of Lassalle," the book that lies
before me as I write.

I have sincere belief in the intuitive perception
of women. I believe that their instinct is stronger
than their reasoning faculty, and that in the great
majority of cases they are justified in their belief,

even if they call it a prejudice. From the beginning of our acquaintance it seemed to me that Lord Haldane would in any large affairs of life be misjudged by his countrymen. In the first place he is a great intellect, and as a nation we hold all knowledge suspect. Secondly, he lacked the proper qualifications of the parliamentarian: he had nothing of the divine gift of push. He did not enjoy the limelight, and as for advertising himself, I think he would not have known how to begin. I do not believe he ever wished to enter the political arena, he never was a politician in the party sense, but he succumbed to the influence of Lord Rosebery and Mr. Asquith who saw that so great an intelligence would be of infinite value to the Liberal party. To me it always seemed a pity to drag the kindly philosopher from his study and to bring him upon the shabby stage whereon the tragi-comedy of party politics is played for the bemusement of the general public. Perhaps Lord Haldane's long and intimate study of the best side of German life led the Liberal leaders to believe that he would be *persona grata* in circles that could curb the worst. Perhaps they too were fascinated by the breadth of his views, the range of his knowledge, the serenity of his outlook, and the clarity of his judgments. There is no doubt that he used all his powers to come to such a friendly arrangement with

Germany as could be reached without detriment to any of the interests of our friends and allies in Europe. There is no doubt that he was face to face for years with the conditions that reached their climax in July, 1914, and that he did all that was possible to preserve peace while preparing for the defence of the country.

Our Tories demanded a scapegoat; the Lilliputians of Westminster and Fleet Street have flung a thousand venomed darts at Gulliver. I am grateful to think that I know the real man whose aspect they have succeeded for a little while in distorting. Quite steadfastly he opposed German militarism, quite hopefully he clung to the belief that he would succeed in his great quest of peace. Perhaps he was too confident. Perhaps he underrated the forces that were opposed to him not only abroad but at home.

We are too near the history of our own time to tell, but I remember one incident that revealed to me the seriousness of the struggle in which he was engaged. There was a meeting to develop the Territorial movement in the county town, and I found myself sitting by his side at the luncheon. Following it he made one of the most stimulating speeches I have ever listened to, appealing to territorials to come forward and prepare themselves to help their country. For simple direct eloquence, for a call to the highest and noblest feelings without one vulgar thought or unworthy expression, I have never heard a speech to equal it. Only a great statesman and a man full of the loftiest patriotism could have spoken as he spoke. Those who are well informed know what we owe to the system of training devised by this lawyer-philosopher and how wonderfully it has borne expansion to meet the sudden needs. His critics have never paused to remember that he was a loyal member of a Cabinet that imposed its collective will upon the people; they have not realised how largely the decisions of the Foreign Office would have availed to control his own views. It is so easy to say that, rather than submit to any reduction of our forces he should have resigned. Those who know Lord Haldane are well aware that pride of place would never have kept him in an office that absorbed all his leisure. Thoughtful people will realise that one of the tenets held by a loyal Cabinet minister is subordination of personal views to the collective views of the ministry. If every man who could not follow his chief along a given road were to resign he would not only lose all chance of giving effect to his purposes but he would make Cabinet rule an impossibility.

While preparing the country for defence, Lord Haldane had to fight the militarism that has at last run wild through Europe; while providing for the

worst, he had, in the highest interests of his countrymen, to seek the best and, if possible, to ensue
it. His Territorial scheme was countered from first
to last by the conscriptionists, they sought by every
overt and covert act to render all his efforts nuga-
tory. I venture to say, not without sound knowledge, that he occupied a position of hideous responsibility with a measure of courage, fortitude and altruism to which those who are best qualified to judge
will always pay tribute. One thing he would not do.
He would not descend into the arena of sordid controversy to gladden the hearts and stimulate the
conceit of petty politicians. If he failed, he was
a glorious failure; but I venture to say that when
the impartial historian, depending on knowledge to
which the general public cannot yet gain access,
surveys the years that led to destruction, he will
rescue Lord Haldane's name and fame from the
accumulation of dirt and rubbish that have been
heaped upon it by men whom none will desire to
remember.

I regard it as a great privilege to know the real
man and to lay my little tribute before him, though
to one so amply dowered with the hate and scorn of
scorn, defenders against such imputations as have
been levelled at him may well be superfluous. But
I owe a great debt to his master mind. Of all the

distinguished men I have been privileged to meet none has had higher qualities of heart and brain, and it seems to me that this is the season in which such a debt should be acknowledged.

XXVI

GROUNDS FOR OPTIMISM

THOSE of us who find in the stress and storm through which the world is passing an irresistible appeal for strenuous action and clear thought, must realise the dangerous tendencies of the time, but it is not right to look upon them as the sum-total of the present upheaval. The present has its tragedies that pierce to the heart of our normal self-restraint; we have to think of the future as well and see whether there is at our door any indication of the unity and brotherhood for which millions have waged a war from which many of the best and bravest will never return. Is there any indication that in the times lying before us, all classes of the community will unite to share the burdens of the State? I think there is.

In many directions the lessons of life and death are not yet learned, but there is one feature of our social life that is truly encouraging. To sum it up in a phrase I would say that people whose example is a considerable force in the national life, have decided that it is neither a vice nor a crime to be poor. A modest establishment in England to-day is more fashionable than an extravagant one; those of us who are burdened by very large places are the objects of sympathy rather than envy.

The flunkey has been redeemed from base servitude, never again I hope and believe, to return. The descendant of Jeames de la Pluche, immortalised by Thackeray, is with the British Expeditionary Force or qualifying to go there. He has discovered that he too is a man. The butler, where he still lingers, is too old for service, the footmen, if any, have been rejected by the army doctor, or have played a part and returned home wounded and unfit as yet for a more strenuous life. They do not propose to remain in a discredited service. Even the maid-servants are reduced to the minimum that is compatible with a fair day's necessary work. The lady's-maid, that last infirmity of conscientious minds, is allowed ample time for helping the nation. The cook gives the benefit of her skill not only to the home but the hospital. The sons of the house are at the front if they are old enough and not too old to be of use, the daughters have found something better than they had imagined possible to do with their time. They have flung themselves as far in the pursuit of duty as they travelled formerly in the pursuit of pleasure.

If one entertains nowadays, it is the working

party or the committee of which one is a member that is received. Simplicity is the order of the hour among friends and one does not entertain acquaintances. The young men have gone from stables and garage, from woods and garden. I think the expensive dressmakers, jewellers, restaurateurs, hairdressers, and the rest of those who catered for the days of our vanity, are having a bad time. I think they will see a worse one. There are still thoughtless women in our midst. I recognise them at once, for they clothe themselves in the furs of harmless animals and wear hats decked with the bodies or nuptial plumage of innocent birds, as if pride of power, vanity, and lust of slaughter had not brought enough injury to the world and vanity must still take toll of life. But these women are a minority and belong to the class that nothing short of ostracism can reach. I think it will reach them, and soon. There has been such an orgie of cruelty in the world of late that the period to be put upon it must be a full one.

The special interest in the changes briefly outlined above, and the list might be continued indefinitely, lies in the approximation at home to the conditions in the field of war. There the struggle for mastery is tending, on every front, to the obliteration of class distinctions. Many of these that in the days before August, 1914, were rigid as

Hindu caste are now dead as well as damned. Mankind has recognised something of its essential brotherhood out there, and now womankind's sisterhood is recognised too. This is almost the more important change, because so many men who remain in England waging the money war that is ever with us are far too immersed in the pursuit of pelf to care about anything else. Against them even our defenders might fail in times of peace if they were left unaided by the other sex. Women have always been the creators and supporters of extravagance, though the fault rests with the men who have until quite recent times refused to allow them any interests that will vie with money-spending and aimless pleasure-seeking. I do not think that even this war could have brought about the change I recognise so gladly and record with so much pleasure, had it not been for the feminist movement. This taught tens of thousands of women to think and thousands to make their thoughts articulate. War faced them with a sense of the value of the work they had undertaken, the urgent need of its pursuit in the interests of the world at large. I feel it is in no small part due to their influence that so much that is unworthy in the life of the modern woman has been voluntarily laid aside and that so much of infinite value has been chosen to replace it.

Just as men have mingled on the battlefield,

women have mingled at home, understanding perhaps for the first time in our social history the viewpoint of classes other than their own, seeing the best in each other's lives and sharing anxieties and burdens as perhaps only women can. But if the good understanding was to be permanent it was essential that privilege should be laid aside. People can enjoy riches without a thought and suffer poverty without a murmur, but contrasts build barriers. It is the sense of sharp contrast that is the undoing of so many girls, that makes for so much bitterness among women. All too often the rich do not understand, the poor are painfully suspicious or self-conscious. There could not be any common meeting ground until all were rich or all were poor. It is not possible under existing social conditions—soon one hopes to be amended—for all to live in comfort. Thank God, it is at least possible for all to be poor.

Not by what we have, but by what we are, let us be judged, and for those who had great possessions there will be a certain satisfaction in the new conditions that money could not purchase.

Flattery, adulation, jealousy, envy, malice and all uncharitableness could be provoked by wealth even though it was wisely dispensed; gratitude was always hard to gain in the genuine form. Love, affection, simple unaffected candour, these were rarely vouchsafed to those whose material prosperity was considerable. It is intolerable that one should patronise or endure patronage, frank and simple relations cannot endure in an atmosphere of inequalities. In England the infection of snobbery was eating into our national life. A considerable section of the press caters for snobs and thrives in the catering. In the United States and in the British Dominions Overseas the state of the public mind is far healthier. It may be that our plight had come about through our insularity, by reason of our super-abundant national riches, by the force of our habit of despising the creator of national wealth and honouring only those who squander it. Whatever the cause the effect was ugly. War has taken drastic steps to abate the evil by depriving of their *locus standi* those who stood for great possessions. They are poorer and better. We shall have a certain number of plutocrats in our midst; out of a war expenditure of four or five millions a day somebody must make money. But the money spinners will find that while the hand of the State will weigh heavily upon them, any lavish expenditure will be eyed askance by the moderate-minded men and women of all classes. The eyes of the majority are opened. Above all, English women of the leisured classes have deliberately laid aside many of the habits and indulgences to which their

practice gave a sanction. This tendency is still in
its infancy, but the tragedy of war has enforced and
will continue to enforce it. All, or at least the
greater part of Europe, after this war will be a
house of mourning. Death leads the van of a procession in which Poverty brings up the rear. As in
a flash the world that lived almost without a serious
care two years ago sees its own real needs and duties
and the terrible inadequacy of the means to fulfil
and perform them.

We find to-day that our national needs are
greater than we knew, our resources less than they
have been for many years. The only true satisfaction to be gathered from the prospect is that we
recognise it. For once in our history it is not left
to a few courageous men to preach an unpopular
gospel in the ears of indifferent wealth and vanity-
stricken fashion. The people who are alive to the
truth of our national state are not devoting anxious
hours to keeping up appearances. Shams that
our life seemed full of so recently, are known for
what they are. For the first time in the social history of our generation it suffices to be an Englishman or an Englishwoman and to have filled the
rôle, however modest, that the fates have assigned
in this world crisis. Shall we miss the old luxuries
of life? Will those of us who accepted them without thought or comment as part of the natural

order of things, forego them without a qualm? I think we shall, because we shall all have a serious and definite occupation. The landowner must develop a good business faculty or go under, the mistress of a large establishment must learn all the domestic arts that her grandmothers practised to perfection or she will not be able to keep it together. The younger sons will not be brought up to look upon loafing as a career, and the girls will be trained to take a part in the world's work, fortified by the knowledge that the State no longer regards them as a negligible quantity. In the near future the British Empire will be demanding more of its sons and daughters and giving them less reward for it, but such a condition encourages the national virtues. We are rather a flint-like people. If we are properly struck we emit light.

Decidedly the world is out of joint, and it is possible to survey the situation and find ample material for pessimism. But we who have made the mistakes or inherited them can set the crooked straight if we recognise the nature of the task. And I see on all sides of me men and women who do. They are preparing the ground on which the virtues engendered by a struggle for national existence may blossom and bear fruit.

XXVII

ANGLO-AMERICAN RELATIONS IN PEACE AND WAR

THE Anglo-Saxon race is on its trial just now, and, however strenuous the times, they do not deny us a measure of leisure in which to estimate the forces upon which we may rely. With battleships and regiments woman has nothing to do, she does but bring painfully into the world those who serve both. It is her mission to shield them with her love and devotion in the season of their helplessness and wait, watch, and pray while the battles join. Hers too it is to do what may be done to heal the wounds of battle, to comfort and to minister, to know the anxiety without the excitement of conflict, to see much of the horror and little of the glory. Yet, far outside the area of strife, woman plays no negligible part in controlling the destinies of nations, for there is a field of social diplomacy in which she labours persistently and the measure of Anglo-Saxon unity that obtains to-day is in no small measure the fruit of her effort.

It will be remembered that before there was an Anglo-American social life, relations between the

mother country and the United States were the
reverse of cordial. Many people in the States regarded this country with suspicion, many in this
country looked upon the States with the contempt
born of ignorance. Emerson, James Russell Low-
ell, Oliver Wendell Holmes, and others helped
Englishmen to understand Americans, but perhaps the best work was done by women. As soon as
they began to understand one another the diver-
gent standpoints were brought into line, old prejudices were seen to lie no deeper than the surface
of things. The freshness and vigour of American
manhood, the honest, unconventional outlook of the
country's womanhood were instantly recognised
when social intercourse had been established and
visitors from the States began to realise that in
coming to England they were but returning to the
land of their fathers. Mistakes are not immortal.
The worst blunderer of a hundred years ago and
the people who suffered most by the blunders have
long been one in the dust to which all that is mortal
of us must return. Latent and underlying sympathies have declared themselves. For thirty years I
have watched the slow conquest of prejudice, the
steady discovery of points of sympathy, the dis-
missal of the old stereotyped ideas that made for
antagonism. To-day, when we are fighting for our
life against a Power that has sworn to dominate

civilisation or perish in the attempt, we find ourselves rich in the sympathy and moral support of all the North American continent, not only the British born of Canada are with us, but in the United States, despite the multitude of foreign influences and the great admixture of interests the general tone is manifestly sympathetic. The German menace has stirred Anglo-Saxon blood throughout the whole world. The observance of a strict and proper neutrality is no bar to American goodwill, our cousins know that this struggle has been forced upon us and that we would have avoided it had not honour forbade.

In the brief intervals of the work of organising the woman's service in my native county of Essex I have been trying to estimate the forces that have brought the changed conditions about, and I think I can see most of them. I have met most if not all the leading men and women of America, both in their own country and here, and no subject has been more completely canvassed in our conversations than the future that the Anglo-Saxon race may hope to share. My views, right or wrong, are my own, and I ask nobody to accept any responsibility for them; if they are correct they should help to explain the present and to indicate lines that the future may follow.

First and foremost among the forces that have

improved Anglo-American relations I place the
Anglo-American marriages that should go far to
improve not only the finances but the breed of our
English aristocracy.   Byron writes of mixed marriages that they "ruin the blood but much improve
the breed."   I accept only the latter proposition.
I think the young generation born of these marriages will be powerful, mentally and physically,
that it may even be in time to stand in the breach
and save the class to which it will belong from sub-
mersion.   Certainly our aristocracy, enfeebled by
intermarriage and circumscribed financially by modern taxation and the depreciation in agricultural
values, degraded by the sale of "honours," would
be bound to go under in the struggle with democracy, and if it is possible to predicate any of the
results of the present cataclysm I should say that
the democracy will issue from it as the dominating
force in Europe.   Another section of a royalty that
tends ever to diminish has been weighed in the balances of war and will, I imagine, be found wanting.

Anglo-American marriages have given our cousins of the New World an interest in the old firm's
business, have made them, even if in a limited sense,
partners in the British Empire unlimited.   I said
as much at the dinner-table the other night and was
promptly challenged until I reminded my critic

that an ex-First Lord of the Admiralty, to whose
genius all, including Lord Charles Beresford, now
pay tribute, is as much American as English. 'Miss
Jerome, Lady Randolph Churchill, was one of the
first recruits to the ranks of the British aristocracy
and has played no small part in English social life.
Winston Churchill has had time to grow up, there
are dozens of Anglo-American lads to whom in the
course of time opportunity will be given. Who
shall say that they too will not prove worthy?

The American girl, married into the wide circle
of Britain's comfortable classes, finds many interests that unite the country of her adoption with the
land of her birth. Visited by her family and friends,
giving introductions for use in the United States
to her husband's relatives, she has been powerful
in spreading social intercourse and in establishing
the vital truth that, in face of many of the great
world problems, England and America see eye to
eye and may work hand in hand. Philanthropy and
social service are the finest solvents of prejudice
between people speaking one language and, when
that prejudice is not founded on fundamental disagreement, and is dependent for its maintenance
upon ignorance, suspicion and the absence of intercourse, it cannot long survive under modern conditions. Every Atlantic Liner is a missionary of
Anglo-American good-will. London and New

York can exchange their thoughts in a few moments, the great sundering force of the Atlantic grows ever less, and the American girl has played a part in unifying Anglo-Saxon thought and sympathy that makes her social reward seem but a small payment for a great service.

Perhaps the great antagonising force in America has been the Irishman. Our administration of the Sister Island has left scars that had been past healing but for Mr. Gladstone and his successors in the office of Liberalism. Happily to-day we stand upon the brink of wiser times, a sane policy has promised to realise the national ambitions of Ireland and a grave danger has united in resistance to foreign aggression the two antagonistic camps. They will meet in the service of a common cause, they will face danger side by side, happily they may learn the full lesson of toleration and mutual respect. It is better I think, much as I hate war, that a thousand Home Rulers and Ulstermen should fall side by side resisting foreign aggression than that fifty should fall in civil strife each by the other's hands. The effect in America of Home Rule, and a union of hearts and hands in the national defence, cannot but be significant. The powerful Irish contingent, as generous as it is quick to anger, almost as prompt to forgive an injury for which atonement has been made as to resent one that is not repaired, will cease to be a hostile factor. Conscious that the old country has done its best to right a grave and lasting wrong, it will forget, as the American born citizen is forgetting, the days of Lords North and Castlereagh. All these quarrels, however serious, have been family quarrels, in the face of foreign aggression the old wounds are healed. I was struck by the splendid action of all parties to the labour disputes when war broke out. In twenty-four hours there were no disputants.

To-day the Anglo-American influences at which I have hinted find no opposing factors in their path. Good will is well-nigh universal, moral support and encouragement are freely ours at this grave moment when we stand so much in need of them. I have always thought, when I have been in America and when I have been entertained by or have entertained Americans at home, that there is a little feeling of pride in the old country. If our short-sighted policy of the third Georgian era turned friends to foes we have paid the price in full and to-day the Anglo-American marriages are giving our trans-Atlantic cousins the material for a noble revenge. They are coming to the relief of the class that persecuted them of old time, renewing its blood, refilling its coffers and preparing through it to administer the world's greatest Empire. It is no unworthy ambition that animates the American girl to-day when she quits the land of her fathers for the land of her grandparents and their forebears, and she has shown herself well able to fulfil it. The pages of Debrett bear witness to what she has done, while those who have been brought into constant and intimate association with her realise that she has shown exceptional capacity in adapting herself to the new environment, in mastering the rather formidable etiquette, in modifying old points of view, and in fitting herself to fill the rather exacting *rôle* she has undertaken.

When I look round social London and see the many-sided work of the American women I feel that they will cover the whole ground. Their energy and resource are admirable and many of their houses are centres of philanthropic as well as social life. Think of the reflex action of all this energy in the States, think of the tens of thousands of American visitors to London in the course of the year and of the hundreds who see English social life as it is and partake of it, and the sympathy and understanding that are ours to-day can be accounted for and understood.

I have long been cognisant of the two great forces that were working, side by side though independently, to destroy Anglo-American friend-

ship. The first was Irish-American resentment, a
perfectly natural expression of feeling. Home
Rule for Ireland was the only possible permanent
cure, and the time for palliatives has long passed.
With the coming of the cure we may look for the
end of the complaint. The other force was more
subtle, and was founded upon the presence in the
States of tens of thousands of the Kaiser's subjects.
They have carried across the Atlantic their old
mischievous motto, "Deutschland über Alles," and
have lost no opportunity of giving it effect. A
powerful press, a great financial group, direct
encouragement from the Kaiser, whose policy—a
relic of Bismarck's day—was to sow ill-will between
Great Britain and the United States under all
circumstances, have been their weapons. To
conciliate the States, to flatter them, to suggest
that they needed German help against British
intrigue, to show their leading representatives
every courtesy, even to affect a sympathy with
democracy, all this was the part of a settled programme. It lacked nothing but success.

This is not the time to go into details of deliberate attempts made to undermine Anglo-
American good will. On a more fitting occasion I
may reveal some. At the moment it does not
seem right to increase the prevailing bitterness,
but I may say that many social intrigues have

come to my own notice and have left me wondering at Teuton pertinacity, at the persistence with which large and small matters alike are pursued, and at the curious psychological failing that nearly always loses count of the human element. Theoretically, logically perhaps, the German advances should have been entirely successful. Unhappily for the Kaiser's ambitions, it was always fairly obvious that behind every courtesy, however extravagant, behind every diplomatic action, however grave or trivial, there lay an Anglophobe bias. It was not perhaps always conscious to its originators; the state of mind towards Great Britain in Germany is largely inherited, and I sometimes think it is well-nigh sub-conscious. Indeed, I would venture the proposition that it is more obvious to an American than it is to the German possessors of it. The United States is of course the world's melting pot; happily for us, and I think for the world at large, the Anglo-Saxon element *is* dominant. In such an environment Anglophobia cannot thrive, and I think the Kaiser's representatives have mistaken the actualities of the situation. Anglo-American squabbles are the little family quarrels with which we are all familiar; if one were to come from the outside and seek to take part in them, he would soon learn that such an intrusion was unwarranted and unwelcome. Instead of extending the area of the original quarrel it would reduce it to vanishing point. In Anglo-American relations the Kaiser must remain an "outsider," accepted while he behaves himself, but known all the time for the representative of a proud, powerful nation that is avid of world power and will shrink from no effort to obtain it, a nation that, if it is to be judged by its rulers, holds that the result justifies the cause, and that kindness, deceit, generosity, cajolery, persuasion, threats, candour, and deceit are all weapons that find a proper place in the armoury of a subtle diplomacy and may be called upon in turn. There is a world in which this standard of things passes current, the world of the company promoter, the international financier, the Jesuit who holds that the end justifies if it cannot sanctify. On the other hand, all these mental processes are abhorrent to the Anglo-Saxon. He is by nature plain and blunt, subtleties are foreign to him. It is his ambition to play the game, and he requires the game to be clean that it may be worth the playing. He likes to place his cards on the table, you will not find them in his sleeve or his boot. We know that the sowing of mistrust between the United States and Great Britain has been one of the chief pre-occupations of German diplomacy, we know too that it has failed as signally as the early and vital attacks upon the Liége forts failed. To accomplish its destiny the Anglo-Saxon race must stand together. We need not interfere in each other's quarrels, we need not model our lives to a pattern that is not sanctified by use and custom, but we will not allow any other nation to come between us and our friendship, or to interfere with that slow, sure growth of understanding and good feeling that may bring to generations unborn the blessing of universal good-fellowship and peace.

In all human probability the Teuton has postponed his own day for generations. The triumphs of more than forty years of peaceful progress have been bartered and have been used as gambling counters, and I believe that a double menace is now in slow course of removal, first from this little island whose sons and great grandsons in their millions are looking, anxious to see how we acquit ourselves, and from those South American Republics that purpose by grace of Providence to work out their own salvation without either the help or the permission of the Kaiser and his legions. When we have succeeded in our present struggle— I do not admit the possibility of a doubt about the issue—the way will be open for the triumphs of peace and for the passing of armaments and tyrannies. Surely in these great changes so long looked for, so eagerly anticipated on both sides of the Atlantic, the whole voice of the United Anglo-Saxon Race will speak in unison. I believe we shall play no small part in the re-shaping and re-building of a shattered and exhausted world, and that the genuine friendliness of our relations will make the task as pleasant as it is responsible. Side by side we have sought peace and ensued it, the overwhelming tragedy may have shown that "man is one and the Fates are three," but it will not alter our national and racial belief that we must develop the tranquillity of the world, that we must develop the arts of peace and arm for defence rather than defiance. Through the gloom and murk of the present hour I find myself looking with assured confidence to the world's future, and whatever the Vision I see the whole Anglo-Saxon race massing irresistible forces for the service of the world.

BIBLIOLIFE

Old Books Deserve a New Life
www.bibliolife.com

Did you know that you can get most of our titles in our trademark EasyScript™ print format? EasyScript™ provides readers with a larger than average typeface, for a reading experience that's easier on the eyes.

Did you know that we have an ever-growing collection of books in many languages?

Order online:
www.bibliolife.com/store

Or to exclusively browse our EasyScript™ collection:
www.bibliogrande.com

At BiblioLife, we aim to make knowledge more accessible by making thousands of titles available to you – quickly and affordably.

Contact us:
BiblioLife
PO Box 21206
Charleston, SC 29413

CPSIA information can be obtained at www.ICGtesting.com
Printed in the USA
LVOW011109121011

250189LV00003B/4/A